# Grandfather's Yarns

## The tales of William Thomas

Edited by Dornie Publishing

## Acknowledgements:

Thanks to the many descendants of the Thomas, Flint and Simon families; in particular Anne-Maree Thomas for assistance with this project. Many thanks to Lloyd Esler for his advice and also for writing the foreword. We gratefully acknowledge the assistance of the Guard family descendants, the Young family, the Palmer family, Kris Herron and the Jillet family, K. Bowden, Kate Stevens, J. Bateman, Curious Expeditions and Tony McGee for sourcing information and images. Kia ora koutou nga Runaka o Oraka/Aparima, Waihopai, Awarua, Hokonui, Otakou, Taumutu, Waiwera. Many thanks to the Southland Museum & Art Gallery (Invercargill), Bluff Maritime Museum, Te Hikoi Cultural Heritage Museum (Riverton), Otautau Museum, Rakiura Museum (Stewart Island), Hokonui Heritage Centre (Gore), Waikawa Museum, Hocken Library (Dunedin), Otago Settlers Museum, Otago University and the National Library of New Zealand. Cheers to Kane Holmes for the insights and whakatauki. Thanks to our friends and families for their encouragement and support.

Dornie Publishing Company
Grasmere, Invercargill
www.dorniepublishing.tk
Original text from the Southern Cross 1894-95
2011 editing © Dornie Publishing 2011
Photographs and images courtesy named individuals or institutions (where known).
All rights reserved.
First published by Dornie Publishing, Invercargill, New Zealand, November 2011.
Second edition September 2012
ISBN  978-0-473-18975-4
Cover design by Strawberrymouse Designs

# EHARA I TE TANGATA KOTAHI ANO I OHO AI I NEHERA.

*There was more than one person awake in ancient times*

# Contents

# Foreword

Every so often you turn a page to reveal an unexpected treasure. Such was my experience when I came across the story of William Thomas, dutifully written by his granddaughter, as he dictated it to be printed as a serial in The Southern Cross. Few of the rough, tough old breed who pioneered the twin industries of whaling and sealing in New Zealand were literate and their tales of adventure and hardship died with them. Oh so rarely does one of them leave his yarns to posterity.

Thomas's story adds a new perspective to Maori/Pakeha relations in the early days of contact and an insight into many of the characters and events that shaped the development of the south of New Zealand.

You can imagine the old man, enjoying the comforts of the modern world, musing on the adventures of the past with its dangers and excitement and contrasting the world of his youth with that of his old age. He sums it up nicely when he says, *"The country was then as wild as you could wish to see it – all bush and swamp. If anyone had suggested that any of us should live to see Invercargill such a town as it is, we should have smiled."*

He would probably have smiled again if anyone had predicted how New Zealand would turn out more than 100 years later.

**Lloyd Esler, September 2011**

# Introduction

*Grandfather's Yarns* is a remarkable collection of true stories as told by an old whaler, William Thomas, to his grandchildren in the 1890s. Thomas's yarns span the course of 90 years and feature many famous (and infamous) personalities, places and key events that helped to shape the early history of southern New Zealand.

Although these yarns were recorded as Thomas remembered them, often many decades after they took place, the historical content is diverse, compelling and surprisingly accurate. He recounts: hardships of a life at sea, daring whaling exploits, shipwrecks, desertions and mutiny. There are some fascinating insights into early colonial social history including: crime and punishment, life in early European settlements, interaction between Maori and Pakeha, and important historical events such the Murihiku Purchase and the Battle of Tuturau. Many of the colourful characters mentioned in Thomas's stories will be familiar to readers with an interest in early New Zealand and Australian history: Bishop Selwyn, Walter Mantell, Tuhawaiki (Bloody Jack), Te Rauparaha, Paddy Gilroy, John Howell, Mike Howe (the notorious Tasmanian Bushranger), and Governors King, Macquarie and Bligh (of the Munity on the Bounty fame) to name but a few. In short, William Thomas's tales are often humorous, sometimes gory, and occasionally tragic; but always gritty, genuine and down to earth.

Before reading these stories it is worthwhile noting the context in which they were recorded. In the early 1890s, after eight decades of vigorous outdoor life, old age and illness began to take its toll on Thomas. It was around this time that he moved from the family home in Riverton to "Herne Hill" farm at Myross Bush near Invercargill. Here he spent the remainder of his days in the care of his youngest daughter, Emma and her family. Indeed, the story of Emma Simon (*nee* Thomas) plays an important role in *Grandfather's Yarns*. At the age of 19 Emma married an Englishman named John Nonnet Simon. Together they had 13 children, a number of whom feature in the yarns[1].   Ever the entrepreneur, John

---

[1] See Appendix 1

was often away with one of his many business interests[2], leaving Emma to run the farm, manage the family finances, and raise the children. She also acted as an interpreter for the Maori Land Court, indicating that she retained a substantial interest in her Maori ancestry, language and culture. With such a hectic workload the added chore of caring for her aging father might have seemed a daunting prospect for several reasons: the Old Age Pension Act wasn't established until two months after Thomas's death in 1898 - meaning there was little in the way of financial support for his care; and, on a less serious note, the elderly William Thomas was reputedly a cheeky character that often gave Emma a hard time about being 'old and crusty'! Nevertheless family records indicate Emma managed well; she was locally renowned for keeping an immaculate house and gardens, and also for being an excellent hostess to the many visitors that came to the Myross Bush farm.

As the indefatigable Emma pressed on with her busy life we might imagine her sigh of relief as the evening came around. The children finished with their chores and the whole family gathered around the fire to listen to the whaling adventures of 'GaGa' William while Emma took a much needed break. Indeed, the grandchildren were most fortunate to have their grandfather as such a ready source of entertainment and information. One of William's older grand-daughters, Caroline 'Lillie' Simon, had the foresight to carefully record these stories and have them published as a series in the Invercargill-based Southern Cross newspaper.

The chapters in this book are arranged according to the original series which ran from April 14, 1894 to its conclusion on May 11, 1895. The text in this book is the same as the original series; however some typographical errors and excessive punctuation have been amended. To provide additional context to the stories I have included footnotes containing extra biographical and historical information.

---

[2] These business interests included: station management at Dipton and Gore, stationery and fancy goods store at Riverton, establishing the *Western Star* newspaper, goldmining, milling, railways construction, butchery, bush clearing, drainage and farming (sheep, cattle and crops).

John Simon and Emma (*nee* Thomas), c.1880s. Courtesy of the Thomas Family.

# Biography of William Thomas & Tukuwaha

William Thomas Junior was born in Sydney, Australia in 1811. His father William Thomas Senior and mother Mary Thomas (*nee* Mason) had moved from England to Sydney in the early 1800s. According to William Junior, his father was "a soldier in the 17th Light Dragoons[3]" and was posted to Australia where he served as an orderly for the various governors of the New South Wales Penal Colony. His service to the governors is verifiable; however William's father was being somewhat 'economical' with the truth about how they got to Australia[4].

William Thomas Senior was in fact a highwayman who was charged on 28 July 1800 with robbery and assault at Hertford the previous month. He was sentenced to death but this was commuted to transportation for life. William's father was then shipped off to Australia in 1802 with 138 other male convicts in the *Coromandel*. William's mother, Mary Mason was tried for larceny in Bristol on 2 April 1803 and then sent to Sydney in the *Experiment* in 1804.

Regardless of how William's parents arrived in Australia they seem to have quickly made the most of their situation. Mary and William met, were married, settled and became well regarded by the local community within a few years after arrival. William Senior did indeed work in Sydney for successive Governors Bligh, King and Macquarie as a body guard and courier for eight years. He was pardoned in 1808.

Of William and Mary's children, William Junior was born in 1811, his brother Charles was a year later, and they had two daughters for whom birthdates and names were not forthcoming. Charles died tragically in 1814 when he was just two years old[5]. It is perhaps in part due to this tragedy that the Thomas family

---

[3] Cyclopedia of New Zealand. Otago and Southland Provincial Districts, 1905. p.1054.

[4] For a full account see *Thomas-Tukuwaha. A record of the families 1834-1984*.

[5] Details for the inquest can be found in Historical Records of New South Wales Series 1, Vol. IX. The Coachman was Joseph Biggs and the passenger was the Governor's wife Lady Macquarie. Also see the Sydney Gazette, 8 October 1814, p.2.

soon relocated to the bustling port town of Hobart, Tasmania in the *Duke of Wellington*.

William's stories of his education and youthful adventures in and around Hobart are a vivid portrayal of childhood in early colonial Tasmania. After his mother passed away, William's father had his hands full raising three children and holding down a job. Subsequently the teenage William took to skipping school to hang out with the rough whalers down at the port. The whaler's tales of adventure must have made an impression on the 15 year old William so in 1826, without the permission of his father, William decided to join a whaling crew. For the next eight years, 'Young Billy' learned his trade in various Tasmanian fisheries. He was soon promoted to second mate/boat steer.

William's first trip to New Zealand was in 1834 aboard the whaler *Mary and Elizabeth*. After experiencing erratic leadership throughout the voyage from Hobart to Otago, many of the crew (including William) decided to desert the captain and try their luck with Joseph Weller's shore based whaling station in the Otago harbour. Here William met with paramount southern Maori Chief Whakataupuka, uncle of the famous southern chief Tuhawaiki ('Bloody Jack'). Although only hinted at in his yarns, William got on very well with southern Maori and was soon married to Tukuwaha, a well born Maori woman, within the year of his arrival.

Tukuwaha was born at the kainga (Maori village) at Wairewa (Little River, Banks Peninsula) around 1816-19. Tukuwaha's mana (status) is hinted at in her whakapapa (lineage). Her parents Makaro and Mokopu-ariki were closely related to the powerful southern chiefs Paitu and Tuhawaiki, and in the 1830s, Tukuwaha's brother Heremaia Mautai became chief of Wairewa.

Although the exact details of William and Tukuwaha's match are unknown, there are several hypothetical scenarios that might account for how they met. As a whaler, William travelled extensively around the coast of the South Island. Often the whaling stations were sited near Maori villages to provide whalers with trading opportunities, protection from hostile Maori groups, and local Maori labour to work in the whale boats. William's first New Zealand employers, the Weller Brothers, had established whaling stations near Tukuwaha's village at Oashore and Ikoraki in 1839; but this was five years after William and Tukuwaha were married. Nevertheless it is possible that they met during William's first expedition to Pegasus Bay, Canterbury in 1834 (see Chapter 3).

Another possibility may relate to the Kai Huanga Feud at Banks Peninsula in the late 1820s. This feud reputedly erupted when a woman named Murihaka casually tried on the kuriawarua (dogskin cape) of an absent chief at the village of Taumutu. This simple action was a massive breach of tapu and could not go unpunished. According to the oral histories, the Taumutu relatives of the offended chief angrily killed two of Murihaka's relations as utu (revenge/payment). When the chief returned, for some reason he decided to punish the people of Taumutu rather than Murikaha. He gathered a war party of warriors from Akaroa and Tukuwaha's village at Waiwera and captured Taumutu. Those survivors from Taumutu sought reinforcements from Murihiku (Otago and Southland) and prepared to counter-attack the settlement at Wairewa. The Murihiku contingent surprised the Banks Peninsula warriors returning from a fishing expedition and engaged them in a one-sided musket battle at sea. With the warriors vanquished the southern group attacked the settlement on shore, killing many women and children[6]. According to tradition so many relatives were eaten that day that the feud was thereafter known as Kai Huanga (Eat Relations).

Back to the story of William and Tukuwaha, this feud provides some tantalising fodder for speculation. If Tukuwaha was, as family records suggest, born and raised in Wairewa, then this would place her at the geographical centre of the conflict as a young child aged between 8 and 10. So how did she survive when so many of her kin perished? Was she sent to her southern relations to avoid being killed or enslaved? Or was she spared or taken hostage by her relation Wakataupuka during the attack? Perhaps her family were simply not in the village at that time. Whatever the reason, both her and her brother at least survived the conflict.

Although the Kai Huanga Feud isn't recounted in William Thomas' yarns, there are some small allusions to it scattered through the chapters. The chief whose cloak started the feud, Te Maiharanui of Akaroa, features prominently in one of

---

[6] Sealer John Boultbee recorded this incident in his journal as taking place around 1827. (Starke 1986:67). One of the chiefs boasted that the Murihiku Maori had killed some 70 of their enemies without loss.

the yarns. William describes him as a "bloodthirsty old villain" that "murdered numbers of innocent people for no good cause whatsoever". Although the context of the yarn relates mostly to the events that led up to Te Rauparaha's attacks on Kaiapoi and Akaroa; William's low opinion of Te Maiharanui may well have been formed through hearing Tukuwaha's stories of the slaughter of her relations during the feud. Te Maiharanui had coerced the warriors of Tukuwaha's village into attacking their own relations at Taumutu, and it was Tukuwaha's village that bore the brunt of the southern counter attack. It is also likely that Tukuwaha's family (and many other Ngai Tahu of the time) resented the weakening of Banks Peninsula Maori through infighting prior to Te Rauparaha's invasion.

Regardless of how they met, William and Tukuwaha were first married in the traditional Maori way around 1834 and then again in a European ceremony during Bishop Selwyn's visit in 1844. The official marriage register records Tukuwaha's name as 'Toogawa'[7]. In total they had four sons and five daughters, and these children also had big families. According to a recent estimate there are around 700 descendants of William and Tukuwaha[8].

William stayed in New Zealand with Tukuwaha and their infant son for the 1834-35 whaling season then went back to Sydney briefly in 1835, probably to tie up any outstanding business and obtain some domestic items to set up his new family. Soon after arriving back in New Zealand in the whaler *Lucy Ann* William and Tukuwaha set up their family home at The Neck, Stewart Island; a small village mostly comprised of European whalers and their Maori wives.

Although the Foveaux Strait whaling industry began to decline from the late 1840s and William officially 'retired' from whaling in the 1850s, he continued to be associated with the sea for the remainder of his working life. Much of his subsequent employment involved transporting goods around Foveaux Strait, building boats, fishing and sealing. One report indicated he was employed

---

[7] Pronounced in the southern dialect. Tukuwaha's name was also variously spelled as Tagawaho, Toogawa and Tukuwoho.

[8] Te Runanga o Ngai Tahu – Oraka Aparima Runaka. Kaumatua linkage and totals. 10 July 2009.

bringing whale oil and bone from Orepuki to Invercargill when he was 62 years old[9].

In 1858 the Thomas family moved from The Neck to Jacob's River (Riverton), just two years after the birth of their youngest child, Francis (Frank). Here, William had better job opportunities with his old whaling associates, such as Captain Howell; and Tukuwaha had family living in the Maori and European settlements. Tragically within three years of their move, both Tukuwaha and young Francis passed away at their family home. The youngest daughter Caroline also died in 1866, aged 12. By this stage however, most of William's family had grown up and were starting families of their own.

William continued on with his business until he retired in Riverton during the 1870s. Little is known of what he did in the 1880s, though we might assume such an active man kept busy in retirement. When illness struck William in the early 1890s he relocated to his daughter Emma's house at Myross Bush. There he died aged 87 on 21 September 1898 after suffering "debilitating bronchitis" for three years.

William Thomas' oldest son, William Junior (b.1835). Courtesy of the Thomas Family.

---

[9] Southland Times (Feb 1, 1873), though this may refer to his son William (above).

1811 – William Thomas Junior born in Sydney

1814 – Thomas family moves to Hobart

Late 1810s – Tukuwaha born at Wairewa, Banks Peninsula.

1826 – William's first season whaling with Captain Kelly.

1827 – Whaling at Adventure Bay with Captain Catlin. Kai Huanga Feud. Te Rauparaha attacks Kaiapoi and Akaroa.

1828 – Whaling at Oyster Bay with Captain Meredith

1829 – William's father passes away. Whaling at Trumpeter Bay for Young and Walford.

1830 – Another season at Trumpeter Bay for Young and Walford.

1834 – William first arrives in New Zealand on the *Elizabeth and Mary*. Deserts at Otago and starts working for Joseph Weller. Meets and marries Tukuwaha, moves to the Neck, Stewart Island.

1835 – Birth of William Junior. William goes back to Australia and returns on the *Lucy Ann*.

1836 – William and other whalers at Ruapuke supply weapons and help ferry warriors across Foveaux Strait to counter attack Te Puoho at Tuturau. The remainder of the year William went whaling at Otago and Port Cooper (Lyttleton).

1837 – Birth of their first daughter Mary. Shore whaling at New River, Invercargill. On board the *Sydney Packet*, the first whaling ship into the estuary.

1838 – Birth of daughter Jane. Whaling at Preservation Inlet on the *Lucy Ann*.

1840 – Birth of daughter Elizabeth.

1842 – Birth of daughter Eliza.

1844 – Bishop Selwyn visits The Neck. William and Tukuwaha are married in the European custom.

1845 – William is First Mate on the *Success*.

1846 – William goes whaling on the *Sydney Packet*.

1848 – Birth of son Charles.

1849 – Birth of son John. William is employed at the Bluff shore whaling station.

1850 – William is First Mate on the *Amazon*.

1851 – Birth of son George. Bishop Selwyn arrives at The Neck on his second visit south and baptises the children. William goes whaling with William Stirling in the *Frolic*.

1853 – Birth of daughter Emma (Emma's children feature in the yarns.)

1855 – Birth of daughter Caroline.

1856 – Birth of son Francis (Frank).

1858 – Family moves to Riverton.

1861 – Tukuwaha and Frank pass away.

1862 – William is recorded as lightering between Riverton, New River and Stewart Island.

1866 – Caroline passes away.

1873 – William lightering whale bone and oil from Orepuki to Riverton.

c.1870s – William retires in Riverton.

c.1890s – William becomes ill and moves to Myross Bush to live with his daughter Emma. Here he regals his grandchildren with the yarns in this book.

1898 – William Thomas dies age 87.

# Chapter 1

## *TUTURAKAPAWA - A TRUE NEW ZEALAND STORY*

"Tell us a story Grandfather please!" shouted a chorus of boyish voices one wintry afternoon.

"All right, my lads," said my grandfather, an old sailor, very good at spinning yarns, and only too pleased to have a listener. "What is it to be about today?"

"Oh, something true," we said, "and something about when you first came to New Zealand."

"When I first came to New Zealand – well, let me see, that was about in '31. Well, I'll tell you a yarn about a Maori chap I knew called Tuturakapawa. He was one of my boat's crew when I was on the *Lucy Ann*[10], in about '38, I think. It was Dunedin – Dunedin not as it is now, but a very rough country, all high flax and manuka, a perfect maze of pig tracks, and very hard to find our way about in.

Well you see, Tuturakapawa had been married (after the Maori fashion) when a baby, to a girl called Ikino. Time passed and she grew into a beautiful and graceful maiden and he, at the time of which I tell you, was in the prime of his young manhood. All went well until a white man named Jim Brown[11], quite an elderly man, an old sealer, fell in love with the youthful Ikino, though she gave him no encouragement, for she was devoted to her Maori lover.

---

[10] A whaler purchased in 1831 by the Weller Brothers of Otago.

[11] James Brown often went whaling with William Thomas and features throughout these yarns. In 1835 Brown was recorded having a very profitable season with Tommy Chasland. They reputedly took a remarkable catch of 15 whales in 17 days at the shore whaling station at the mouth of the Mataura (near present day Fortrose).

But jealousy – that passion which is said to be as 'cruel as the grave[12]' – stepped in, and one evening, towards dark, in Brown's hut. The two men – the Maori and the white - both a little groggy, came to blows about the girl.

Tuturakapawa, hitting in his anger and at random, smashed a window and cut his head with the broken glass. Now, a Maori particularly dislikes to have blood drawn from (or did in those days), especially about the head; and now the fierce unreasoning passion of the native was fairly roused, for he blamed Brown for the accident and rushed from the hut to fetch a musket. Having obtained one, he rushed back to the hut, but a well meaning Yankee carpenter, who did not realise the awful depth of the Maori's rage, would not let him enter – but stood in the doorway, thinking to prevent the man from doing anything in the heat of his anger for which he might be sorry afterwards.

Tuturakapawa could see his rival passing backwards and forwards in the hut behind the Yankee, and, watching a chance, fired but missing the intended mark, shot the carpenter dead.

At once a hue and cry was raised for the Maori murderer, who had escaped into the bush. But no trace of him could be found – the undergrowth was so dense that none but a native could find his way about with a great amount of ease, and if any of his tribe did know the whereabouts they kept it to themselves. For some time this went on, the white people in a great state for the capture, but all in vain.

At the time there was a French whaler in the harbour – Captain Le Bas[13] in charge and when attempts to catch Tuturakapawa had failed, the French captain told the whites that he'd get their man for them without even leaving the ship. They were astonished at that and wondered how the "old man" would manage it.

The old chief Taiaroa[14] was in the habit of going aboard the whaler on friendly visits to dinner etc. One day he went as usual to see the French captain. After dinner, the captain ordered his mate to bring the "bracelets" and fasten them on

---

[12] Song of Solomon 6:8

[13] Le Bons Bay (The Bones) on Banks Peninsula was named by Captain Le Bas.

[14] Te Matenga Tairoa (c.1795 – 1863). Leading chief of Ngai Tahu. From Ngai Te Ruahikihiki and Ngati Moki hapu.

Taiaroa. Of course the old warrior, as became his blood, objected to this strange and unexpected behaviour on the part of the captain; but some of the crew being called, the old fellow was soon reduced to order – and put in irons.

'Now Taiaroa,' said the captain, 'do you see my yardarm there? Well I'll take you out to sea and hang you there, and then hand you over to the hungry fishes, unless you tell your people to bring in the Maori who killed the white man, for I'm sure they know where he's hiding.'

Of course the news that old Taiaroa was a prisoner on board the French whaler travelled quickly ashore. The Maoris did not like the idea of his suffering for the guilty man's sin, so they brought Tuturakapawa in - not that they had any difficulty in doing so, for he gave himself up quite willingly when he heard of the state of affairs.

They brought him to Captain Le Bas, thinking he wanted him but he told them to hand the prisoner to the whites as it was their affair, and nothing remained for to do but release Taiaroa, which he did.

Tuturakapawa was in a room in the house of Mr Weller with a sentry in guard, till convenient to hand him over to the law at Port Nicholson. One day the sentry Steve Murphy was pacing up and down the front room where Tuturakapawa was confined when he saw approaching a beautiful Maori girl whom he instantly recognised as Ikino.

Tuturakapawa begged that his "wiena[15]" might be allowed come in to see him, and Steve seeing no harm, consented. They talked in loving whispers for some time and seemed extremely sorrowful and affectionate so Steve left them to themselves. "

Presently the Maori called it to him 'Steve, lend me your gun.'

'Oh, no, me hearty,' said Steve 'you'd shoot ME!'

'I swear I won't, and you know I won't Steve,' answered the Maori.

---

[15] Wahine – wife, woman.

'All right,' said the good-natured but careless Irishman and handed over the weapon.

Steve continued his walk and had almost forgotten the gun incident when he heard a loud report, and rushing in to the room he saw a sight which froze his blood. The Maori girl sat against the wall with her arms classed tightly around the waist of her lover. He held the gun with the muzzle close pressed to his breast, and had fixed the trigger with his toe. The ball passed through his heart and hers, and there were the murderer Tuturakapawa and his faithful Ikino - dead[16].

"Well, I think he was a wicked man, Grandfather," said gentle little Bertie, the youngest of the group after a thoughtful silence.

"He certainly was not a good man my son," answered Grandfather, "but you must remember that he had never been taught to control his naturally violent temper in the least, and he loved the girl so. All love is selfish lad, and the wild

---

[16] McNab 1913 p.285-6 relates a slightly different version of this story.

*At Otago, during the month of February* [1840], *an incident happened which threw the whole settlement into a state of extreme excitement. The son of a chief named Bogana* [Tuturakapawa] *retired on board a whaler, which lay at anchor in the bay, and remained drinking for some time. He was very drunk when he came ashore. About an hour after his arrival, and before the effects of his drinking bout had worn off, he went to the house of a man named James Brown, but becoming very abusive, was ordered out. Refusing to go, harsh measures had to be employed, and, in the scuffle, a pane of glass was broken and a piece of it struck the Chief. This roused his indignation and he hurried to his house, armed himself with a loaded musket, and returned to Mr. Brown's house. When he presented the gun at Mr. Brown, a man, who was standing near, pushed the gun to one side, and the contents were lodged in a young man, a carpenter, who had formerly belonged to the Mechanic, of New Brunswick, killing him almost at once. When Mr. Weller learned of it he had the murderer confined and a guard set over him. Shortly afterwards a loaded musket was passed in to the Maori, by someone unknown to the guard, and, getting his wife to sit behind him, the Maori put the muzzle to his breast, and his toe to the trigger, and one shot ended the lives of both.*

*The unfortunate thing was that two perished, and the Maoris, thinking that satisfaction should be obtained for the death of the wife, turned their attention to a scheme for revenge. Brown grew so alarmed at the local feeling that he pleaded with D'Urville the commander of the Astrolabe, when in Port Otago, to take him away. In view of the circumstances, and of the fact that he was a good Maori linguist, the French Commander gave him and his wife a passage to the Bay of Islands.*

Another version was related by John Hunter in the *Evening Star* (Dunedin) 26 October 1884. Hunter recalled that on 15 February 1840 Teuteraki Pauwa (*sic*) had quarrelled with Brown, who owned a grog shop. Apparently Brown pointed an unloaded pistol at Tuturakapawa and told him to leave. Tuturakapawa withdrew but returned with a loaded musket and shot at Brown through a window, accidentally hitting the carpenter. He was immediately put under arrest until someone would take him to be tried in Sydney. The manner of death for Tuturakapawa and Ikino corresponds exactly with Thomas and McNab.

passionate heart could not bear to think of anyone else as his Ikino. I was a young chap at the time myself, and there was not one amongst us who did not think he died game, and the noble devotion of the Maori girl touched the hearts of many an old salt."

Weller's Whaling Station on Otago Peninsula, mid 19<sup>th</sup> century. After A Coville.

# Chapter 2

## *The First Land Sale in Otago.*

"Another yarn," said my Grandfather one evening as we boys gathered around him, clamouring for a story, "Well, well. I suppose I must tell you one," he said a little testily though we knew that he was only delighted to do so.

"Well, I've just been reading about the land sales they've been having here lately, when not even the timely jokes of our auctioneer could provoke much of a bidding[17], and it reminded me of the first land sale ever held in Otago, when they sold the land from Taiaroa Heads to Nugget Point 60 miles along the coast 10 miles inland, I think they called it[18].

The money had been sent out from England to pay for the land. I can see it all now – Mr Mantell standing behind a table, on which there were three white-duckbags[19], marked with plain figures - 1200 on two, and a third bag contained that number of hard gold sovereigns.

It was a beautiful day, and a goodly number of both Maoris and whites had gathered from all around the district, to see how the money would be distributed.

---

[17] William is probably referring to the sale of the Ocean View Estate near Fortrose recounted in the Southland Times 2 April 1894. The auction drew a large attendance of 200 people but there were few takers for the property. The auctioneer Mr J.A. Mitchell found his usually persuasive combination of "badinage and humorous rail" was ineffectual. The newspaper suggests that the terms for purchase were too hard; the developers essentially asking for cash up front.

[18] The signing and purchase of the Otakou (Otago) block deed took place on 31st July 1844 between Ngai Tahu and the New Zealand Company (directed by Edward Gibbon Wakefield). Thomas seems to have confused Mantell, who supervised the signing of the Murihiku Block sale in 1853, with one of Symonds, Tuckett or Clarke who oversaw the purchase in 1844.

[19] Canvas or calico bags.

Mr Mantell held up the first bag marked 1200 and turning to the chief Bloody Jack[20], asked him what he was to do with it.

Jack told him to count out 300 sovereigns for Taiaroa, which he did, and it was laughable to see Taiaroa yelling and dancing and capering about with the money in his hat. Next Jack ordered 300 more to be given to Kuriti[21] (Jack White) a cousin of Taiaroa's. From 300 it dropped to 50. A few received 50, then others got 20, 10 and 5; according as Jack thought they deserved it, till Mr Mantell had only a handful of coins left. These Jack told him to give to boys, which he did, two and three according to size. Some of the young rogues, after receiving their share would dodge in out amongst the crowd, and then come and out their hands for more. Mr Mantell would not have noticed, but Jack saw them and soon put them to the right about.

I remember one old woman with a baby boy on her back, held out her hand for something for the baby, but Mr Mantell had to put it into the baby's own fat fist for Jack, not being in present Parliament[22] did not believe in woman's rights and never gave property of any kind, land or money, to a woman.

Jack then took the other two bags for himself. He told the Maoris that he would have taken it all, for it was all his by rights, only that their forefathers had so bravely killed the tribe known as the Katimumu[23]. Not a single voice did the Maoris raise against the decree of the chief – no strikes and socialism then, my boys!

"Why did they want to kill the Kaitmumu for?" asked Fred.

---

[20] "Bloody Jack" aka John/Hone Tuhawaiki (born c.1800 – died 1844).

[21] Karetai (born c.1800 – 1860)

[22] New Zealand women were first given the right to vote in 1893, just a year before this story was recounted.

[23] Ngati (Kati) Mamoe.

---

"Well, you see, the Katimumu had killed Jack's father or grandfather, Kuwiriri[24], while the tribe was out looking for food, though I believe there was some feud between that. When Jack's tribe, the Kitau[25], heard about it, a number of them gave chase to the Katimumu and followed them up the mountain known as East Dome[26]. Now, the Kitau had very little food with them, and were unprepared for a long stay - not so the Katimumu, and so the Maoris say they had a wizard in their tribe who caused a mist to lie on the mountain, so that the Kitau lost their way, and died of starvation. Then the remainder of the tribe did their best to slay every Katumumu they could catch, and to this day they are thought very little of by the Maoris[27].

I know that on Crawfish Island[28] where they are prospecting now, in the caves (of which there are a good number and some running in a considerable distance, and dark as the grave too) there bones of many a murdered Katimumu."

"Bloody Jack must have been a hard case to receive such a euphonious nickname," observed Fred.

"I don't know," said Grandfather, "why they gave him such a name, for he was not a very bloodthirsty man. He was very fond of painting himself with red orche, so perhaps that it[29].

---

[24] Tuhawaiki's ancestor was Kaweriri, a famous Ngai Tahu warrior who was killed in one of the last major battles of the 18th century between Ngai Tahu and Ngati Mamoe. The battle took place by the Aparima River, near Riverton in Southland.

[25] Ngai (Kai) Tahu

[26] About 20 kilometres northwest of Waikaia, Southland.

[27] William is relating the conflict between Kai Tahu and a rebel faction of Kati Mamoe, eventually leading to the legend of a "Lost Tribe" of Maori living in remote areas of Fiordland.

[28] Crayfish Island, Dusky Sound, Fiordland. Rich gold finds in the quartz deposits of Crayfish Is. were reported in the *Southland Times* (March 12, 1894, p.3) however the lode was limited and quickly worked out.

[29] According to legend, Tuhawaiki learned English from the sealers and whalers arrived in Foveaux Strait in the early 1800s. He most likely picked up the nickname from his frequent use of the word "bloody" rather than from any overt bloodthirstiness.

I'll never forget the first time I saw him. We were down at the heads at Dunedin, one morning, on board the *Mary Elizabeth*, the boat that I came to N.Z. in, Jack Hughes, one of our men, said to me, 'Here comes Jack.'

I looked, but could only see some men getting into a boat on shore. Just then I had to go below for something, but as the Maori boat neared the ship I could hear the men on deck explaining to those who had not been there before, which was Jack and who the other men were.

I was anxious to see Jack, for I'd heard a lot about him, so I hurried up on deck. Just as my head appeared above the companion-way, my noble Jack stooped and snatched my hat off, and put on his own head. It was a large Panama hat with a broad, black ribbon, so it just suited the chief, for the Maoris, even to this day, particularly value black ribbon.

But only to see him! The figure he cut. It would frighten any of you. He was painted from head to foot with red ochre, and had one side of his head as close to cropped as a newly shorn sheep, whilst on the other side, his hair stuck out in brushy abundance. He wore only a mat and looked a tremendous height.

He was a very good-looking man though – if his face had not been tattooed so hideously, for he had a splendid figure. Once, when he went to Sydney, the officers in the barracks there gave him a Captain's uniform, almost new, and 15 or 16 suits for privates. He was greatly pleased and when he came home, chose his men and rigged then out in all the glory of their regimentals[30]. But one Christmas they were having great games, and all the soldiers got drunk, so Jack punished them by putting them in the 'black hole' of Rhuapuka. Now this black hole was a potato pit, and the men looked 'beautiful' when they were released in the morning.

But to return to my hat, I was going to try to recover it, but Jack Hughes advised me to let him keep it, so I went below for another, when I came up again, Jack saw that I meant to let him keep the hat, and he came patted me on the back to thank me for it. Our Skipper was frightened of Jack. He wouldn't have denied him anything he asked for on the brig. I know he used to tremble till Jack went

---

[30] In June 1840, Tuhawaiki and his men boarded the H.M.S. Herald anchored off Ruapuke to sign the South Island version of the Treaty of Waitangi. They were all in full dress uniform.

ashore; but he need not have been so frightened, for Jack was as harmless a man as one could meet. He was the best native I ever knew, and a good deal better than some white men, too.

He was a great favourite, was poor Jack, for unlike most natives he never begged and he was very generous, too. I didn't lose by giving him that hat, for a few days afterwards he brought me a splendid mat, and he was always trying to load me with presents after that.

Now boys, I can't tell you any more tonight; but some other day I'll tell you more about Bloody Jack, or Tuhawaka[31] as I think his name was, if you care to hear."

Drawing of Tuhawaiki's moko (facial tattoo), 1840.

---

[31] Tuhawaiki.

# Chapter 3

### *WHALING REMINISCENCES – A CALL AT PEGASUS*

"I have promised to tell you a yarn about my first voyage to New Zealand," said Grandfather, "so I'll do it now. We sailed from Hobart on April 2$^{nd}$, 1831, on board the whaler *Mary and Elizabeth*, owned by Capt. Kelly the harbourmaster at Hobart[32]. That night we went down to Hull Bay, about 11 miles down the river, and took on some wood, iron poles and about seven sheep.

Next morning we put out to sea and our owner left us. I remember, he shook hands all round, and wished us a pleasant voyage; but he hadn't been gone a quarter of an hour before the captain[33] was quarrelling with the first mate and for such a trifle too. I had been looking through the spy-glass and handed it to the first mate saying 'Here Tom, take a last fond look at the she-oak on the hull,' which he was doing when the captain came up. And didn't he go on at the poor fellow; but Tom never answered him a word.

The glass always hung in the companion, and we frequently used it. I wonder what he would have said if he had caught us using it, for I was only second mate[34]. That night it commenced to blow. As they were recoiling the top sail the captain called out to a new hand, named Chaffey[35], to take in the jib. Chaffey told him if he wanted his jib taken in he could not do it himself. They had a fearful

---

[32] It was actually 12 April 1834. The *Mary and Elizabeth* whaling articles were signed on 31$^{st}$ March 1834 by owner James Kelly and James Lucas. William Thomas was recorded as a Boatsteerer on the Fortieth Lay. Interestingly for a man who had been educated, he signed with an 'X' indicating his mark.

[33] Captain W. Lovitt

[34] Boatsteerers were generally second mates.

[35] Zachariah Chaffery.

row over it, but as Chaffey was not booked as an A.B.[36], the skipper could not force him to do it.

You see, we did not commence our voyage very amicably, but the skipper was an unreasonable old tartar_____ dyspeptic, I suppose.

On 9th April we anchored in Pegasus[37], and there we lay for five days, pulling about and looking for a whale, but never a one did we see. One morning we thought of leaving Pegasus and hove short. As they were loosening the topsails however, one of the men called out 'Here comes a canoe!' I ran up the mast, but I could see that it was a dingy, and no canoe, and I said so to the captain. He declared it was a canoe, and swore at me roundly. As they came closer we could see it was a white man and two Maori boys and a dog standing for'ard in the boat, which in the distance had looked exactly like another man.

Our men were frightened of the N.Z. natives, and were much relived when they saw a white man in the boat. You see, very exaggerated accounts of the bloodthirstiness of the Maoris had reached us. The party in the boat were very kind, and insisted on giving us a pig, which the captain sent me ashore to bring to our boat.

From Pegasus we went to Otago[38], and it was there I first saw Bloody Jack[39], as I told you the other day. Our skipper was frightened of the natives there and he went off to Cloudy Bay. He had been there on two previous occasions."

---

[36] A.B. – Able Seaman

[37] Pegasus Bay north of Christchurch.

[38] According to the official reports, when the ship called at Otago her boat, gear, and dead whales were seized by local Maori, and they only managed to escape by a "precipitate retreat". As Grandfather recalled, the local Maori were friendly and they had caught no whales at Pegasus to seize! Perhaps Captain Lovitt's official report was a 'creative rendering' of the actual events for insurance purposes. In Lovitt's defence however, William late recounts another captain warning Lovett of impending hostilities and at the time the southern tribes were gathering for a military expedition against Te Rauparaha in the northern South Island. McNab 1913, p.71-2.

[39] Honi/John Tuhawaiki

"And what did you do there?" asked Fred.

"Bless you, my boy! I didn't go with him. I ran away – in fact most of the crew did. Mr Weller came aboard our boat one day. It was very wet, and in the evening he wanted to know if we would take him ashore, which we did, and he invited the whole boat's crew up to his house. As we were all wet, we did not go then, but rowing back to the ship, all the fellows were saying what a nice man he was, and they were all eyes to go and see him. So one night we took the boat and went on shore. Mr Weller gave us food, tea, pipes, tobacco and grog. All the men thought him a perfect angel compared to our skipper, and wanted to leave the ship at once, but I told them they could run away if they liked but not when I was in charge of the boat; so I took them all back to the ship. I believe some of them got ashore again that night. I had promised Mr Weller that I would go whaling with him, so I waited for my chance to get away. One day Captain Hayward came on board. Our skipper gave the steward orders to watch us, and he was aft doing so. I got one of the men that came aboard with the captain to keep the steward in a tank, and we managed to pass a rope along and haul Captain Hayward's boat under the bows. We had our swags in the forecastle, and were on before the steward noticed. He saw us for a moment, though, and notified the captain, who came running up and told us he'd fire if we didn't come back. I very bravely told him to fire, as I knew as well as he did that there were no arms on board. He didn't make any effort to capture us, because Captain Hayward had gone aboard to warn him that the Maoris were talking of taking the brig, and so he was only too anxious to get off.

It was a beautiful night, and when we got ashore the first man we saw was Wakataupuka the chief of Rhuapuka. He was standing on the bank and as we came up he sent a Maori woman down to learn our business. We couldn't make her understand very well, but she somehow satisfied the chief, and he treated us very kindly. I gave the Maoris a pound of tobacco to take to Capt. Hayward's boat back to the *Mary and Elizabeth*.

The Wakataupuka told the Maoris that they could take the brig if they liked, but if they did he would take all the provisions out of Mr Weller's store and go with all his people to Rhuapuka; so when the white people came after them for taking the brig, where would they be without provisions or arms. So they gave up the idea. That night, much to our joy, we saw the brig go out about ten o'clock[40].

Next day I met Joseph Weller, and he told me to send for the allowance for all the men, just as the others did, which I did; but all the men wished themselves back on the ship when they saw what it was, for there we always had as much as we could eat. Seven pounds of flour, one and a half pounds of sugar, and 10lb salt junk[41] for each man was all we got. It was about the usual allowance then, I think, but we thought it was very poor. However Joe Weller was a splendid fellow to work for – a gentleman, every inch of him. Everyone trusted him, his word was as good as all the black-and-white in creation of most men, and whatever he promised he fulfilled to the letter.

One day, we were after a whale. My boatsteerer had just fastened to him and I was going for'ard to kill him, when the next thing I knew I was in the water, but I was better off than the others for I was hauled into another boat before some of the others came up at all.

The chaps in the other boat, who were a short distance off, said that the whale leaped right over our boat, lashing left and right. It knocked the boat to pieces. The Right whale always has a white parasite on its head, and one fellow who had on a blue shirt was covered in this white substance, so he must have been pretty close quarters to the whales head. The same whale stove in Jack Hughes boat too, after they lanced him out, the lance killed him.

After that season, I went to Sydney and the next winter I whaled on the *Lucy Ann*[42]. In the winter of '36, when we were whaling again in Otago, the schooner, *Joseph Weller*, came from Sydney through Cook Strait. Ned Weller was aboard her, and he brought news of his brother Joseph's death. He sent me to Port Cooper (Canterbury) in charge of three boats, but it was too late in the season, and we

---

[40]From Otago, Lovitt set sail for Cloudy Bay then sailed back to Derwent near Hobart arriving July 9. Lovitt was relieved of his command and the *Mary and Elizabeth* returned to New Zealand later on with a new captain.

[41] Salted beef or pork.

[42] In 1835 under Captain Anglem. William was married to Tukuwaha and had William Thomas Junior by this stage.

only got three whales. We went ashore at Port Cooper. There was a Maori lying ill in a cave. He had been shot by a man on the *Lucy Ann* which was on her way to Sydney by this time[43]. The man said he was firing at a bird on the beach, the Maori was whaling on the beach and received the whole charge upon him. The gun had been loaded with a bullet cut in two, and one half had gone through the Maori's cheek, lodging in his jawbone. That half had been extracted, but the other half, after striking the other cheekbone and knocking out several teeth on that side, had sliced off and worked its way down through the flesh on the poor man's neck. No one would take it out for him, so he asked me to do it. I was frightened to at first, as it was so near the jugular vein; but he would have it, even after I had explained the danger to him. He was as cool as anything while I was doing it. It came out right and hardly bled at all, and he was soon sound again.

"I wish you would tell us something about the old times at Bluff, Grandfather." said Fred

"So I will tomorrow, Fred".

---

[43] The *Lucy Ann* was under Captain Bruce at this time. He reported that the natives were causing trouble at Port Bunn, Cuttle Cove, Preservation Inlet (McNab 1913:93), so it is possible that the crew were anxious about any perceived aggression by Maori soon after.

Edward 'Ned' Weller (1814-1893).

# Chapter 4

## OLD WHALING DAYS AT BLUFF – ADVENTURES ON LAND AND SEA

Next day we reminded Grandfather of his promise to tell us something of when he was whaling at Bluff.

"Promised to tell you something about Bluff?" he said. "It must have been in weak moment, but you boys gave me no peace."

"Well, the first time I went there was in '37. We were whaling in shore parties at the New River[44] and often rowed down to Bluff. It was not much of a place then I must confess. I wasn't there very often until I went to whale in the *Success* in '43. That season we got a Sperm whale[45] off the Solanders, a Right whale[46] at Preservation, and another one just outside Bluff, by the point. One of the boatsteerers, a Maori named Tapui, fastened to it, and John Topi killed it. I told Toi, the headsman of the third boat, to tow in the whale as long as it was flood tide, but as soon as it began to ebb, to anchor it if he hadn't got it right in, and to take it in in the first flood if we hadn't got back before that.

Just off Barracouta Point[47] we saw another whale, and the second boat fastened to it, but they hung too short. The whale stopped dead, and the boat ran right into it and was smashed, but not badly, though. The whale bounded through the water till it got to a mile off, and there it lay knocking furiously about. We towed the damaged boat ashore. Then I tried to persuade John Topi to come with me to get the whale. The Maori's begged him not to, but I soon got him around, and he agreed to row me close enough to lance it.

---

[44] Sandy Point or Omaui, near Invercargill.

[45] Sperm whale - *Physeter macrocephalus*

[46] Southern Right whale - *Eubalaena australis*

[47] A rocky headland 4km south of Omaui, near Invercargill.

Well he did, and soon the whale was spouting blood. Sometimes the lance is sudden death to them you know, but at other times they live for hours, and then they make the white water fly! Next day we got both the whales into Bluff and cut them in."

"What's that?" we all inquired.

"Why, 'cutting in' a whale is cutting them up to the bone and blubber. We used to anchor the whale close to the ship and then run out a small stage. It was done with four double blocks and tackle. When they fixed the hooks into the blubber, and those on board heaved, the whale turned slowly round. That's what they called worming it. The man on the stage has a spade made for the purpose to peel off the blubber as the whale turns round, and thus they heave piece after piece into the ship. We had no way of utilising the carcass in those days and just let it float away.

Cutting in a whale, c.1903.

I'll never forget the second season I went whaling. I was boatsteerer and old Griffiths was the headsman. I was only a young lad then, just 19. I was standing on the whale as we were cutting it in. As they were heaving up the first piece of blubber, the fall broke and down came the blanket piece, as they call it. Luckily for me, in falling, it first struck the side of the ship, but it came onto the whale with sufficient force to send it reeling over. I went right to the bottom, and both saw and felt it, but come up quite unhurt. All on board thought I must be killed, but the blubber had not even touched me. I came up under the bows and was steadying myself with one leg over the bobstays while they were looking for me.

But I meant to tell you about Bluff, so I must not wander from my subject. There were a lot of wild cattle about Bluff then, in the bush just beyond Ocean Beach. Johnny Jones brought them there and gave them to his brother-in-law, Dick Sizemore, but he didn't want them, so Jones gave a third to Mr Spencer and a third to Bill Stirling, keeping the rest to himself. One night about nine o'clock, Bill Stirling came aboard with a cow's tail. We all wanted to know what good it was, but he said he only brought it to convince us that he had shot a cow, as otherwise we would have declared he was dreaming. So next morning we set off to find the cow, but we wandered about the hush for hours and never saw sign of it. At last a Maori found it and we cut it up and carried it back to the boat.

Going back the tide was out. We had left the boat a good way out and waded ashore. Crossing that mud flat we managed to strike a strip of sand with little shells sharp as needles. The loads we were carrying made it no pleasant task. I remember, one chap did swear. We used to have great sport cattle shooting then. One day we were out, Archie Davis shot a tremendous bull. Another chap and I were about 100 yards from the high water mark in the boat, and the bull rushed into the water within a foot or two of us. But just as we expected him to charge us, he changed his mind and tore back to the shore. Just beyond high water mark he fell dead. He was a tremendous beast. When we cut him up he weighed considerably over 10 cwt[48]. It was just opposite the Bluff where we got him.

Next year I went with Captain Howell in the *Amazon*. We did not whale long, but went for timber for the new boat he was building in Jacob's River. One day we were leaving the Bluff bound for Codfish, Captain Howell sent me ashore for

---

[48] Roughly 500kg.

one of the men we left behind and some grog. So off we started, Dr Richards, two others and myself in a four oared boat. We took some seal skins and fish to pay for the grog.

Well we got our man and the grog too, and we went out to overtake the ship. Some of the men had had a glass too much. 'Old Davy' I remember was very merry and was singing as one of the crew, an Irishman said, 'like a *nartingale*.[sic]'

When we reached the schooner, she was in the rip. That rip isn't much to look at, but it's the very mischief to get into. However, the doctor, one of the men, and myself managed to jump on to the schooner's deck; but the others, with happy old Davy, stayed in the boat and I thought they would be tossed on deck, boat and all.

I said to Captain Howell, 'We'll have to get out of this, skipper.' So we ran her inside the rip into smooth water, hoisted the boat up, and beat out. We were soon outside then.

There were about 21 men on board and by night they were nearly all drunk. The cook made some soup out of a quarter of beef that Mr Spencer gave us, and 'Long Harry' walked right into the copper. Of course it took him about up to the knee and he was very badly scalded."

"You didn't eat that soup surely?" we all cried.

"Eat it! Of course we did. An Irishman, 'Jimmy the Sawyer' made us all laugh, for he swore he'd eaten Harry's slipper."

"Off you go to your lessons now boys. I'll finish telling you about the Bluff some other time."

# Chapter 5

## *A SULKY WIFE - SMOKING HER OUT*

"Now, now, boys! Stop wrangling and come here and I'll go on with the yarn I was telling the other evening," said Grandfather. So we quietly settled down to hear what he had to say.

"In '45," he continued, "I was again first mate on the *Success*, and headsman of the first boat. Towards the end of the season we went down to Waikouaiti with our oil and bone and brought back a cargo of gear for Captain Howell's new boat.

On our way back we called in at Port Molyneux[49]. You boys have all been there, I know, but in those days there were only two white men there – a Mr Russell and a Mr Wiltshire. I don't know who Mr Russell was, but the other was a gentleman very highly connected. You know Wiltshire Bay down there. Well, that's called after him[50].

They were in partnership, and had a good deal of land there. I've heard that they argued and quarrelled about everything; but they never became angry or rude, and always addressed each other in the most ceremonious and courteous manner."

"I wish Jack would take a lesson out of their book," sighed Fred, who had just been called all the "Daisies" and "Chumps" in Jack's vocabulary.

"Oh, you needn't talk, Mr Goody-good!" began Jack, but Grandfather interposed, saying:

---

[49] Near the present settlement of Kaka Point, South Otago. Wiltshire Bay is 1.5 kilometres south of the settlement.

[50] George Wiltshire (sometimes spelled Wilsher).

"Why boys, I thought I was to tell you a yarn; but it seems you want to have that quarrel over again."

"Oh," we all cried, "go on Grandfather, please!"

"Well," continued Grandfather, "we went ashore at Port Molyneux, and took a present of rum to the two gentlemen. Of course, they were delighted to see us, as they did not often see anyone there. We were in Mr Russell's house, and he began to tell us in his slow, grandiloquent style, something about his friend and partner. You see, Mr Wiltshire had married a Maori woman named Matumukiriri, a lady of somewhat uneven temper. One day she took the sulks with her husband and escaped up the chimney. There she sat on a beam, and all the poor man's pleading could not bring her down. It was a huge wooden chimney the whole width of the room. She was a big woman too, and she sat there and would not move. It must have been a comical spectacle, to see the fat, sulky woman on her sooty elevation, and her lordly spouse in beseeching attitude on the floor. When all his pleading proved in vain, in desperation he sent for Mr Russell.

'And,' said the old gentleman, 'I soon upset her stolidity, and she made a rapid, though ungraceful, descent.'

You see, Mr Wiltshire had not thought of smoking her out, but as soon as she was down he said in the meekest of tones:

'Will you have a little arrowroot, my dear?' The very idea. Idea!

(Left) Makariri (Makareidi) daughter of a local chief who kept house for Wiltshire.

The disgust expressed in the old man's tone at the weakness of his friend sent us off into roars of laughter. It did not take much to raise a laugh from us in those days. We had not much to laugh at as a rule. He saw that we enjoyed his yarns, so he went on for a long time. He told us that Mr Mantell wanted him to move off the land he occupied as it was thought to be a good site for the township. 'But,' said Mr Russell, 'I said to him: "Mr Mantell, I brought this land legally from Bloody Jack in Sydney, and I won't shift. Of course, you could burn me out, but I know her Majesty Queen Victoria would not commit arson."

While he was talking to us, two of the boys belonging to our ship went and sucked all his eggs and put them back in the nests. Of course he found out and blamed some of the Maoris, but he never suspected our boys, although the young rascals had done it right enough.

We got back to Bluff late the following afternoon. As the schooner ran into the place where she always lay the skipper dropped the anchor, and as she ran out again she fouled her anchor in the chain.

I thought there was something wrong, and told Ned Kelly to come ashore for me if it commenced to blow in the night. So the lad did. He told me that the schooner was dragging.

Now she wouldn't have dragged, only the skipper hoisted the mail topsail when it commenced to blow – for what I don't suppose he knew himself. The sail soon filled and shifted the schooner, and by the time I got on board she was some way down and bumping on the rocks. We ran out the boats, but it was no use and she was soon dashed to pieces just where the Pilot Station is now. Of course no lives were lost, but very little of the cargo was saved[51].

That season we had on board an old chap who used to tell a yarn about seeing an eclipse of the sun. They were out somewhere to the no'ard of the North Cape, on their way to New Zealand in about '35[52].

---

[51] This took place around April 1845.

[52] They were possibly in the middle of the New Year's Eve eclipse of December 31, 1833. It lasted for five minutes, 35 seconds and was at its darkest just off the north of the North Island.

'One morning,' he used to say, 'we were pretty slack and some of us were skylarking about. It was a lovely morning, the sun was out, and it was beautifully warm. All of a sudden the sky grew hazy and it got thicker and thicker. One said one thing and another said another. But it grew darker and darker. The sun disappeared altogether and the stars came out and it was bitterly cold. I can tell you it was enough to frighten anyone who had no idea of what was up,' he used to say, when we smiled in a superior way.

'We looked at each other with ghastly faces, and some of them began to pray – a thing they hadn't done for many a long day. By golly,' the old man used to say, 'there was not much skylarking then. I rushed down to the cabin. The skipper was lying on the couch, and as soon as I came near the table he said,

'What's the matter Bill?'

'Matter,' I said, 'you come on deck and see what'll be the matter with you! Why Black Dick and Bo'sun (two Australian blacks they had on board) have both turned white.'

The skipper laughed and laughed, and I saw him glance at the nautical almanac. Then he explained to me that it was a total eclipse of the sun, I rushed up on deck again to relive the other poor chap's minds, for they were terribly frightened.

"The old man was very fond of telling us that yarn, and we often heard it. That's enough for tonight, boys. Some other time I'll finish telling you about when I was whaling at Bluff."

# Chapter 6

## BLUFF REMINISCENCES - A COW WITH TWO HEARTS –

## "THE HOLE IN THE WALL" – BURNING OF THE OCEAN CHIEF

A few days later, after a good deal of persuasion on our part, grandfather continued his story about the old whaling days at Bluff.

"In '49," he said, "we whaled in shore parties at Bluff. We did not do very well though; the whales were beginning to get pretty scarce about there. I remember that season; Mr Spencer gave a chap who was whaling with us permission to shoot a cow. The rogue went off and shot two and caught a calf as well.

Next morning he got some of the other men to help him bring the beef over to Bluff. He didn't want it to be known that he had shot two cows, and was going to throw one of the hearts away; but the man he gave the other heart to said:

'Don't throw it away – give it to me.'

'Oh no.' said the chap who shot the cows, 'the women will see it and then it will come out that I shot two cows.'

'Oh trust me,' said the other, 'I'll see to that.' And he got the two hearts.

Well when he took the two hearts home, his wife, who was a Maori woman said:

'Boy shot two cows eh?'

'Oh no,' said her husband, 'the cow is not like us you know; a cow has two hearts.'

And the woman believed him. One day nearly all the women in the settlement were up at Mr Spencer's. They were jabbering away and in the course of the conversation something was said about cows.         The woman I told you about announced that cows have two hearts; then they began to argue about it and appealed to Mr Spencer, who told them that a cow only had one heart, and asked what they wanted to know for. Of course the woman who had made the statement wanted to justify herself and said:

'Well, the cow Boy shot the other day had two hearts – I saw them myself.'

'Oh the villain, he shot two!' said Mr Spencer.

He was rather fond of the chap, though, and did not do anything to him. He was a grand old chap, was Jimmy Katore, as they called him, and very generous."

"What did they call him that for?" we all inquired.

"Well, you see," continued Grandfather, "he wanted to bring needles and fish-hooks, and such things as he thought the Maori needed and exchange them for fishing lines and flax. He always used to tell them he had '*katore*[53]' – everything, it means, I think. So they gave him the name of Jimmy Katore.

Well when I was first mate of the *Amazon* we got three sperm whales I think it was. We towed them to Breaksea Sound; it is such a beautiful land-locked harbour. There was a place we went into that season. They called it the 'Hole in the Wall'. An old Maori called 'Old Mike', who died afterwards on Centre Island, showed it to us. A stranger might go there a thousand times, and never see it; it looks just like a crack in the cliff, but on looking closer you can see it's a good-sized opening, and inside there is a sheet of water. There used to be a good number of seals in there in the old days. You can only get in, thought when it is dead low tide and smooth water.

The season after that I whaled with Bill Stirling in the *Frolic*. We got three sperm whales there too. Stirling died at Bluff about that time, and was buried over at Tewais Point[54]. The *Frolic* was sold to Captain Howell. He whaled her for a season and then went to Sydney.

---

[53] Mea katoa – everything.

[54] Stirling's grave is on Tiwai Point. Stirling Point in Bluff is named after William Stirling.

I never went whaling after that, though Captain Howell wanted me to go with him in the *Eliza*. But I wanted to stay ashore, and wouldn't go. He was a grand skipper, and we always had a good time with him. The men all liked him, because he never put them on an allowance. They were allowed to help themselves to anything on the ship, the only condition being that they were not to grumble if the rations ran out.

I will tell you about the *Ocean Chief* being burnt at Bluff. It was in 1862, I think[55]. I was lightering in a schooner called the *Caroline*, belonging to Captain Howell. As a rule, we brought timber from Stewart Island to New River and then took goods from Invercargill to Riverton, to Blacklock and Calder's Store. In those days the nearest road to the Lakes was from Riverton. Of course there were no trains then – everything was carted in wagons, so you see, there was always plenty of trade between Invercargill and Riverton. Well, this trip we were taking a cargo of wool from Invercargill to the *New Great Britain*, a ship that was lying at Bluff.

Just before we left the wharf I went to the Customs house. I was talking to Captain Elles, and he came out to the door with me.

'Look,' he said, 'whatever is that smoke?'

'I don't know,' I said, 'but it is coming from the direction of Bluff.'

'But there's nothing at the Bluff to burn like that; I wonder what it can be,' said the captain. Shortly afterwards I sailed away. We got outside the Bluff about five o'clock, but it was ebb tide and we could not get in. We could still see great columns of black smoke rising, but could not think what was burning.

At midnight we were able to get in, and then we could see that the *Ocean Chief* was on fire. It was burning brilliantly, and we could see all the other ships as plainly as if it had been mid-day. It was a grand sight, though – the tongues of flame darting and leaping and casting their flickering shadows all around that great hill looming in the background; and every now and then there was a tremendous splash and swish as the ship gradually went to pieces, and the

---

[55] 2 January 1862.

burning fragments fell into the water. But grand as the sight was, we were too tired and wet to watch it long. We ran the *Caroline* close up to the *New Great Britain*, so as to be hands to unload in the morning, and then we went to bed.

Next morning we went ashore and had breakfast at Hughes Eagle Hotel. Mr Price, the magistrate, and one or two policemen came down in the course of the day, for, you see, they thought the ship had been set on fire on purpose. They suspected the ship's carpenter, because there were holes drilled in an arrangement they had for pumping the ship and dousing the fire at the same time, and when they had tried to use this they found that it would not work.

The court was held outside the hotel on the grass. All the people of Bluff were there as well as the sailors from the ships. The sailors of the *Ocean Chief* were tried too. You see, the saloon had been elaborately decorated with mirrors and pictures of considerable value. When the fire was discovered they slung these, and somehow, in putting them into the long boat, they slipped and went with a run and nearly all were smashed and damaged. Of course the sailors were blamed for carelessness, but the captain of the *New Great Britain* spoke up for them and asked how many officers there were on the *Ocean Chief*. The captain told him four.

'Well,' said he, 'what were they doing to leave a parcel of drunken sailors to look after valuable property? They are the ones who ought to be blamed,' and that cleared the sailors."

Breaksea Sound, c.1905.

# Chapter 7

## THE FIRST SCHOONER IN THE NEW RIVER

"Yes, yes, so I did boys," said Grandfather this afternoon when we told him he had promised to tell is about the first ship that ever came to the New River[56]. "There was nothing extraordinary about it, only that it WAS the first ship that ever came up here, so I hope you are not expecting anything exciting," he said.

"It was in '37. We were whaling in shore parties at the New River[57] and a schooner came in March. Its name was the *Sydney Packet*. Of course we boarded her, and when she dropped her anchor and the sails were clewed up, Captain Stewart Bruce ordered the steward to bring up the grog, and treated all hands. An Irishman belonging to the ship flourished his glass crying:
'Here's to Port Palmer and the River Tay!'

You see the cunning chap thought that by saying this he would get another glass, because Ned Palmer, a part-owner, was on board, and Captain Bruce was a Scotchman, so he named the river Tay out of a compliment to him. However Paddy's christening did not stand, as you know.

The year before we were in Otago (Dunedin) on board the *Sydney Packet*[58]. One day Captain Catlin came to us for help. You see, he had run his brig (the *Genii*) ashore in Parakanui Bay[59]. The sails were all set when it happened in the dog-watch between six and eight in the evening; but when they touched bottom, instead of doing anything to try and get her off, he lowered the boat and went off to try and get help, leaving the first mate in charge.

---

[56] Now known as the Oreti estuary, beside Invercargill.

[57] The whaling station was at Oue, Sandy Point.

[58] September 1836.

[59] Purakaunui Bay, west of the Otago Heads.

When he got into Otago Harbour, he first went to Mr Weller, then to a brig called the *Nimrod*, and then he came to the *Sydney Packet*. The captain of the *Nimrod* and all the men in the cabin of the *Sydney Packet*, except Captain Jimmy Katore and myself went with him. He had been rowing about in the harbour for over an hour, and then he stopped to buy some grog, and again to get a keg of water.

Jimmy Katore called out to him: 'You're a bright captain, you are, with a ship ashore, and here you are fooling away the time. First you get rum and then you get water to cool your coppers, and very likely your ship is going to pieces all the time.'

When they reached the place where the *Genii* went ashore, not a thing was to be seen. They rowed about for hours, and when it grew dark flashed lights about. The brig was safe. The mate, Bill Gully, after the captain left, turned all the water casks, which were kept on deck, bung downwards, and let the water run out. This lightened the ship considerably, and a breeze just then setting in from the land, the ship soon floated off. Gully told me afterwards that he saw the lights, but would not make any sign. He said that if he had been able to navigate the ship, or if there had been a navigator on board, they would not have waited for the captain at all, but have gone straight to Sydney. Next morning the captain and others saw the *Genii* and boarded her. When Gully told them how he managed to get her off, Captain Bruce said:

'You must have been very careless to let her go ashore?'

'Who said I let her go ashore?' said Gully.

'Why, your Captain said so,' answered Bruce.

Gully never said another word, but went to the cabin where Captain Catlin and the others were. Going up to the captain he said, 'Did you say that I let her go ashore on my watch?' The captain could not deny it because so many had heard him. Gully took hold of the unfortunate captain's nose and wrung it.

'You scoundrelly liar,' he said, 'you know well that YOU ran the ship on shore, and on purpose too, you old villain. You see, gentlemen,' turning to the others, 'Captain Catlin has made a very bad voyage, and he is ashamed to go back to Sydney. All his crew that were on lay wages have deserted and the present crew are on monthly wages, so you see he would not have been sorry to lose the brig[60].' This may have been so, but when they went back to Sydney, Gully was tried for wringing the captain's nose, and he lost all wages and his lay as well through it."

"I don't understand what a lay is." said Fred.

"Well it is very easy to understand. If they had a share, they got a certain amount of everything that was got. Some had a fifteenth, others a twentieth, and so on. They worked for this instead of wages. If the voyage was a good one, they all did well, and if nothing was made the crew got nothing. That year the *Sydney Packet* was to take us all down to Rhuapuka[61]. As we were starting one afternoon, there was a heavy tide on and the schooner missed stay. Ned Palmer[62] called out to Bruce to try her again. He did, and missed again, so he tried to veer her round. She was almost round when her stem caught in the rocks and she stuck. They lowered a boat under the bows to run out the kedge, but there was such a ripple on that they were frightened of upsetting the small boat. There were a good many women aboard, and they were all frightened. My wife[63] threatened to jump out and swim ashore; she was a good swimmer, but I knew she could not do that, so I got John Topi, Harry Fife, and two others of my boat's crew to help. We lowered a five-oared boat belonging to Jim Brown, and we were off without being noticed by anybody.

---

[60] Later voyages were more successful; on 23 November 1836 the *Genii* brought 1000 barrels of black oil, 50 of sperm oil and two tons of bone to Otago.

[61] Ruapuke Island, Foveaux Strait.

[62] William 'Ned' Palmer – successful whaling entrepreneur

[63] Mary/Tuhuwaha

When I was coming back I could hear them saying to one another, 'Who took Jim Brown's boat?' and when I went on deck the captain told me I had no right to take it. I told him that I had told Jack Owens to come with his big boat to haul the *Packet* off, and that he and seven or eight men were coming at once. The captain changed his tune and thanked me for my thoughtfulness and promptitude.

That was not really what took me ashore, as I told you, but I thought I'd take the praise for myself, as the accident wouldn't have happened, only the captain was rather groggy, and I thought in his present condition he'd never get the schooner off, so I conducted myself as though I had done something very virtuous, when in reality the thought of bringing Jack Owens to the rescue only suggested itself to me when we saw his boat as we went ashore.

Nine men came in the big boat and they soon hauled the *Packet* off. Ned Palmer was on board, and he promised the men five gallons of rum for saving his ship for him. Palmer was a very mean man, but the men knew him well enough, and they were determined to keep him to his word, and at daylight next morning, just as we were heaving up anchor, they came alongside. Then Jimmy Katore came to the rescue.

'Captain Bruce,' said he, 'fill up these men's keg and I'LL pay you for it, and if no one pays me I'll report you to the underwriters, and then the insurance agent will pay me.' He said this to frighten Ned Palmer. You see, the *Sydney Packet* had been ashore several times, and neither Palmer nor the Captain had reported it, as they ought to have done, so if Spencer were to carry out his threat they would both get into trouble.

The men got their grog. When they found it was the real thing, they gave three cheers for good old Jimmy Katore.

# Chapter 8

## *"OLD JOCK" - THE BEST SCOTCHMAN I EVER SAW*

"Well, well boys, if you must have a yarn, I'll tell you about an old man I was whaling with in Preservation once.

His name was John Wilson, but he was generally called Old Jock. He was an elderly man when I first saw him – an Edinburgh man – and the best Scotchman I ever saw. I never saw him to know who he was till one night in '37, when we were whaling in the New River. It was very dark and we had gone to bed early. Suddenly I woke up and heard someone stumbling over our whalebone. I woke my mate and told him I thought someone was stealing our bone, and we were just getting up to see when a knock came at the door of the hut.

When we opened it, to our surprise in walked Captain Lawson and John Wilson. Old Jock introduced me to the Captain. I had not met either of them before, but Jock said he knew me well by sight, having often seen me in Hobart. Then I remembered having seen him. He was working with some Scotch stonemasons, building a large store, which was afterwards taken over by the government.

Wilson had been transported when very young. He told me about it once, though it was not a subject he loved to dwell upon. He was only a boy at the time – in fact, little more than a child – and he happened to be in a crowd of machinery breakers[64], and they were, every one of them, arrested and sent out.

Captain Lawson told me that a boat crew of his had run away from Bluff and he was after a man named McKenzie, whom he heard was working in our fishery, and presently in came the second mate with poor Jim.

---

[64] Luddites - a group of British textile artisans that protested the increasing industrialisation of the early 19th century by breaking machinery.

He was a grand little fellow, was Jim, and the only civil darky I ever saw. The captain held out his hand and said:

'What made you run away, McKenzie?'

'Well,' said Jim, 'It was too much pulling about from daylight to dark in these bays on a pound of bread and a pound of salt junk a day, and I couldn't stand it.'

'But you'll have to come back,' said the captain, 'you signed for that amount, and it's not my place to break through the agreement, though I would if I could.' They stayed yarning for about half an hour with us, then I put them on board their vessel, which was lying about a mile down the river.

Oh I forgot to tell you the vessel's name – it was the *Bombay*, of London, and that year we had our fishery just near the Pilot Station now stands. The next day I think it was, it began to blow and the *Bombay* was driven ashore, and there she stuck for six weeks, and every time the wind was from the S.W. she got pretty well knocked about[65]. There were no rocks there or she would have gone to bits, but instead she just mumped about on a gravelly bottom.

One day all the captains came over from Bluff to see what they could do. They tried to heave her off with two anchors, but the bottom was nothing but shingle, and each time up came the anchors clean and shiny. They tried again and again, but always with the same results.

A man named Adderly, the second mate of the *Margaret Wryatt*[66] and I were standing by the fore rigging of the *Bombay*, and he said, "Have you ever been there?" pointing to an ugly looking rock in mid-stream. I told him I'd never been there.

'Well,' he said, 'call your Maoris and let's go and have a look at it.' So we did, and when we were coming back he said, 'I could get their ship off for them.'

---

[65] The *Bombay* sailed from London 24 January 1836 and was grounded 7 May 1837. When the accident happened the Bombay had 300 barrels of sperm oil, 100 barrels of black oil, and two tons of whalebone on board.

[66] *Margret Rait*, an American whaler.

---

'Could you?' I said, 'How?'

'Why, put the chain round that rock and heave her off,' said Adderly, so I advised him to tell the captain. Now Adderly was a nice enough man when sober, but he was a terror on the drink, and he said:

'Oh they would never listen to an old drunkard like me when there are so many captains aboard.'

When we got back to the *Bombay*, I saw Captain Lawson a little apart from the rest – the quarter deck was full of captains – so I beckoned to him and told him Adderly's plan. He went to the others and told them, but they all cried it down and said it would be impossible, and how could they carry the chain out there? However, next day Adderly said to me, 'Let's ask Captain Lawson to try what I suggested. There are the *Bombay's* boats, four boats from Bluff, and your two.'

So we took out the ship's chains, shackled a smaller chain round the rock and fastened the two chains together, and at a signal those on board heaved at the windlass, and off she came flying. That rock has been called the Bombay Rock ever since, I believe[67]. But dear me, I meant to tell you more about Old Jock. That same year he came into the New River on board the *Lynx*, which came in for our bones and oil. After she was loaded up they lay there for a night, and next morning when they were unmooring her, she got on a sand-spit and was wrecked[68]. Next season I was in Preservation with Old Jock, and he told me a great deal about his former life, but we'll put that off for another time.

---

[67] During the rescue the *Bombay* lost 70 fathoms of chain and 20 fathoms of stream cable, she also lost two bower anchors and one stream anchor. Captain Lawson's diary entry can be read in McNab 1913:181-2, though he gives no reference or credit to Adderly's plan.

[68] The *Lynx*, owned by Johnny Jones and captained by J. Gauson, arrived at the New River whaling station on 22 October 1837. There they took on 100 tuns of black oil. On departing for Sydney on November 18, they were towed out of the estuary but ran aground three miles out. The wind shifted and caused the *Lynx* to become irreversibly stuck. About 6 o'clock a boat from the station came out and rescued the crew from the wreck. Almost nothing was saved from the wreck. (Sydney Monitor December 23, 1837). Local folklore implies that the crew of the *Lynx* had been heartily imbibing the local distilled cabbage tree whiskey - Owen McShane's famous "Cooper's Schnapps/Chained Lighting" before the accident.

# Chapter 9

*OLD JOCK'S ADVENTURES.*

*LEFT ON THE AUCKLAND ISLANDS – SEALING WITH CAPTAIN ANGLEM*

"Old Jock used to tell us that in 1825 he sailed with Captain Lovett in the *Sally*, to seal at the Auckland Islands. One day when they were out, they lost a boat's crew. It seems that rounding a certain point there is a dangerous channel, and unless you get through with the tide, it is all over for you. When the wind and tide meet there it is a terror.

This time they were all out – the *Sally* had two boats' crew. Captain Lovett went first with his boat and was carried through all right; but the second boat missed the tide, and not a trace of men or boat was ever seen again. That season another sealer named Jack Guard persuaded Old Jock and a man named Bill Shaw to leave the *Sally* and join him, which they did. The *Sally* had to go back to Hobart then, because she was too short-handed to seal.

Towards the end of the season, Guard found a tremendous lot of seals. He couldn't get them then, but determined to come back again the next year. When he made his find he would not take Old Jock and Shaw with him, for fear they would sell the information to someone else, and also he was a little afraid of getting into trouble with the owners of the *Sally*. So Guard and another man got the two men ashore on some pretext or other and left them. And there they stayed several months. There was nothing to eat but seal – when they could get that – for Guard left them no provisions. Of course there were plenty of muttonbirds, but they did not know how to catch them. The place they were in was somewhere near Sarah's Bosom[69]. They had a fire, and they found a piece of

---

[69] Sarah's Bosom (now known as Port Ross) was where the survivors of the *General Grant* (wrecked May 1866) made their camp for 15 months. The survivor's stories echo the depravations faced by Old Jock and Bill Shaw.

iron on which they used to fry their seal, and one day they found an old quart pot. They had only one knife between them; it was a long knife used for skinning seals. You can imagine how wearily the time would pass for the poor fellows, sometimes starving and nothing to do except get wood to keep up the fire.

Towards the end of their stay there Bill Shaw took very ill, and Jock was most anxious about him. He used to go down to the beach and gather little fish about two inches long, boil these, and give Shaw the water to drink. Poor chap, it was about the best he could do.

One day, when he was down on the rock getting these fish, what should he see but the jib-boom of a vessel coming around the point! He rushed up to the sick man and cried – 'Oh! My God, Bill Shaw, here's a ship!' With that, he said, Bill jumped up as if nothing were the matter with him, and ran down to the beach.

They watched and saw the ship drop anchor, and then they recognised it as the very ship that left them there.

Presently a boat was lowered and as he saw who they were, he sharpened his knife and said to Shaw: 'If ever man was killed, I swear I'll kill those two men the minute they land.'

But Bill Shaw dropped on his knees, clasped his hands, and begged and prayed of Jock not to do it.

'If you do Jock, they'll hang me for it as well as you.'

Jock always said though, that if ever man meant murder in his heart, he did that time, and he never gave himself any credit for not committing it, always declaring it was for Shaw's sake.

Jock sealed with Guard for some time after that, and then they went with him to Sydney. A few seasons after that he went sealing to Chatham Islands in a big boat with Captain Anglem.

One afternoon towards dusk they saw a number of seals on a reef, and someone suggested that they should haul the boat up and stay there till morning. They did so, but in the night a gale set in from the N.W. and their boat was smashed to pieces, only the bows remaining on the reef. The gale lasted for three days, and at high water they had to tie themselves to the reef to avoid being washed away. At low water Captain Anglem used to read prayers, and Jock said he never felt like despairing until one day Black Bosun (a Sydney black) said to him:

'Oh Jock, you pray for me. I can't pray.' He said then that he broke down and cried like a child.

It had been dreadful weather, but that day Black Bosun declared it was breaking. None of the others could see that it was, though they tried very hard to think that they did; but at 12 o'clock, sure enough it did clear, and at low water they stretched some of their skins, which had been washed into crevices of the rocks when the boat broke up, over what was left of their boat, and in safety they all reached a small island not far off.

The first thing they saw on landing was a large seal. Bosun killed it and Jock was sent to skin it. One man had a little dry powder, but it was very hard to get alight. Just as Jock was thinking of having raw steak off the seal, he heard welcome news:

'Bosun's got a light!'

"There wasn't a stick of wood on the little island," continued Grandfather in his story about Old Jock. "They had to keep up the fire with blubber, and after a while, of course the stones got so hot that is was easy enough to cook. Captain Anglem went all over the island, which was very small, and counted the albatross, and they were put on an allowance of half an albatross a day. When they killed an occasional seal, of course that was extra food.

There were nine of them altogether, I think, and three Maoris among that number. They cut out a big hole in a bank of soft rock, and into this they plucked the feathers of the birds. I should think the hole resembled a baker's oven over more than anything else; but into this they all crept at night, like pigs into straw.

Of course they had to keep warm and that was the only way. They had very little clothing between them all. Captain Anglem often told me that in the mornings when he came out of this hole he literally had to scrape the vermin off himself. All the clothing he had was the lining of an old monkey jacket, and that was green baize. He often said that he must have been the picture.

Captain Anglem was very anxious to get back to the main island, as he had left his wife there, and so, after they had saved up enough seal skins, they again rigged the boat up, and Captain Anglem said one night that if the next day were fine they would make an effort to reach the island, which was about 16 miles off.

But the morning came, to their dismay they found that the boat was gone. The Maoris, who heard what the captain said, and fearful of being left behind, had gone off in the night with the boat, and they got safely to the main island.

Somehow it seemed to the poor fellows that their last hope was gone with their boat. But after some time, when some more skins had accumulated, Captain Anglem made them into a kind of canoe by stretching them on albatross bones.

*Oh dear me!*

*'Twas a thing beyond description –*

*such a wretched wherry,*

*Perhaps ne'er ventured on a pond,*

*Or crossed a ferry.*

It was such an uncertain affair that none of the others would venture with him, so the captain went by himself and he reached the island in safety. But sad to say, when he got there, he found that his wife was dead. The Chatham Islanders told him that when she saw the pieces of the broken boat come floating in, she gave up all hope of ever seeing him again; she never ate nor drank afterwards, and in a day or two died of a broken heart. There was very little food there, so Captain Anglem went back to the others in his miserable little skiff, much to their joy and delight.

They had been on the island for about five months when one day Black Bosun declared he saw a sail. All the others looked, and for some time they could see nothing, but at last they saw a ship apparently making straight for them. Presently they saw two boats close at hand, coming straight to the island they were on.

'Now,' said Captain Anglem, 'we'll have to plant, for if they see us they won't land, for of course they will guess at our condition and think we'll want to go in their ship.'

So they all hid until the sailors landed, and then they showed themselves, and they presented such a spectacle that the sailors almost fainted. Some of the men made different noises and nearly frightened the newcomers into fit; but Captain Anglem called out:

'Don't be frightened, sailors; we're Englishmen like you are.'

In the scuffle and fright of the strangers, Jock rushed down to the water's edge and jumped into the first mates boat.

'I can't take you my men,' said the mate, 'we've two shipwrecked crews aboard now.'

Jock said, 'Nothing but death will take me out of this boat. You can kill me if you like.'

The mate saw that they were in earnest, so he offered to take one man aboard the vessel to see what the captain would say. Jock said, 'You go Captain Anglem. If the man's got a heart to soften, you can do it.'

The captain was very angry with the mate for not bringing them all, and sent back at once for them. When he saw them and what a pitiable condition they were in, he actually shed tears and kept saying,

'My poor men! My poor men!'

He ordered gruel to be made for them, but they didn't wait for the gruel – they were too hungry for that – but devoured biscuit and fat pork till they couldn't eat anymore. They were given clothes and hot water, and everything that was done for their comfort was done.

When Jock had washed and shaved, and put on a decent suit of clothes, he came upon deck. 'Bless my soul' said the captain, 'I thought you were a regular old man, and you're quite a young one.'

The captain and all his crew were Yankees. He took the castaways in his vessel, the *Rob Roy*, to Pegasus, where he landed them and gave them provisions. Jock used to say he never saw a nicer or kinder old man than the old captain.
And now, boys, I think you ought to be satisfied for tonight."

We all thanked him, Fred declaring that Captain Anglem was a 'stunner'.

Sarah's Bosom (Port Ross), Auckland Islands, c. 1840. After Le Breton 1842

# Chapter 10

## IN PRESERVATION INLET – TAKEN AT WORD – THRASHING A BOY TO DEATH

"Grandfather, do tell us another story please," said Bertie this afternoon, and we all gathered around grandfather's chair to hear what he had to tell.

"Well boys, I was just thinking of a dreadful thing that happened once when we were going into Preservation Inlet. It was '36, I think. We were going in the *Sydney Packet*[70].

There was no wind. So Captain Bruce fired off a small cannon that he always had on a swivel, as a signal for the boats on shore to come out and tow us in. Twice he fired, and still the men on shore did not seem to have heard, for there was no sign of their coming out to us.

There was an old English man-o-warsman aboard, and he said to the captain, 'Let me load it, (and with a fearful oath) I'll make them hear or go to h___ with the report.'

He loaded the gun, touched it, and the next instant it burst with a fearful explosion and shattered the man to pieces, and strange to say, though there were ever so many of us standing quite near at hand, we were all untouched. We gathered what remained of the poor man into his hammock, though it was ghastly work, and while we were doing so we saw the boats coming out from the shore.

---

[70] During this time many of the crew of the Sydney Packet were in varying stages of recovery from contracting influenza in Sydney. During the stopover at Ruapuke they inadvertently passed it on to the Maori population who were preparing to respond to the invasion of Te Rauparaha and Te Puoho. Newspaper reports of the time suggest that 600 southern Maori died from this new strain of the flu. Although this figure is probably exaggerated, the Maori population was severely diminished.

When they towed us in we dragged the body to the top of a nugget just off Crayfish Island. On reaching the top of the rock we found there was scarcely enough earth to cover him. However we managed to bury the body. Captain Bruce refused to read prayers over the man. I can tell you boys, as tough and all as some of the men were, that man's sudden and terrible death impressed them all, and there was not nearly so much cursing and swearing done for a long time among those men.

They had a bad time of it altogether that year at Preservation. I was not there myself, for I went to Bluff, but I have often heard about it. The man at the head of one of the fishing boats thrashed a boy to death there! That frightened all the whalers away, as the Maori's say, for though they were often caught there before, there was never seen one there afterwards.

It happened in this way: three chaps were out in a boat one day – a Maori named Moot, an Otaheite man, and a white boy[71]. They stopped to put the Otaheite man ashore to get some woodhens. When they landed him there was a nasty sea running and a high tide; and when they went to get him again the boat somehow ran off a big wave into the rocks, and was smashed to pieces in a minute.

They had to walk back to the fishery. Arrived there, they told the owner of the boat[72] that it was all the boy's fault that it had been lost. Of course it was far more Moot's fault that the boat had been lost.

The man flew into a terrible passion, and taking a rope, thrashed the boy till he was senseless, and then chucked him outside into the rain, telling all hands that if they dared to go near him he'd make them suffer for it.

That man was simply drunk with rage. Once the poor boy said, 'Oh don't beat me any more sir. I'll work for you my life to pay for the boat.'

---

[71] Charles Denahan aged 18 or 19.

[72] The owner was Edward 'Ned' Palmer (b.1810- d.1896)

'Oh you wretch,' cried the man, 'your life would not pay me for the boat.' And he forthwith thrashed the boy harder than ever!

"How could others stand by and let him behave like that?" said Fred.

"I don't know," said Grandfather, "but they did. I don't think they were all there, but I suppose they daren't interfere. The masters had more absolute command over the men then than they have now, you know.

The Maoris occupied one half of the hut they lived in, and the white people the other. In the night the Maoris heard the groans of the poor boy, so they went out and found him lying in the pouring rain, soaked through. They brought him inside, took off his wet clothes, and wrapped him in a blanket, and put him close to the fire; but the poor boy never regained consciousness, and the next day he died.[73]"

Edwin 'Ned' Palmer, c. mid 19th century. Courtesy of the Young family.

---

[73] Denahan was beaten with a 2 ½ inch spliced rope on June 14 and died of wounds on July 4, 1837.

*AN UNWILLING HOSTESS – HOW SHE WAS OUTWITTED –*

*MORE ABOUT OLD JOCK.*

"After the season was over at Preservation Inlet," continued Grandfather, "they all went back to Sydney. A man named Jim Davis[74] reported the boy's death officially, and the man was arrested. But he was very rich and had plenty of friends. He was allowed to come to New Zealand to get evidence for his side, and he collected seven or eight men, some of them ignorant Maoris, and others unprincipled whites. He had to pay them well for their services, too, £3 a month all the time they were with him, besides board and lodgings, and he was to pay them a lump sum down if he got off. Then he paid Jim Davis' mate £40 to leave the country, so there was only one witness left against him. I remember seeing the whole case in the papers[75].

All the men swore that the boy died by 'visitation of God!'[76] and as there was not sufficient evidence against the man, of course he won the case. Then the lawyers wanted to have Jim Davis up for perjury[77], but the Judge wouldn't hear of it, saying that he hadn't the least doubt of the man's guilt, and that he was sorry that the evidence was not sufficient to convict him. I always felt sorry for that man though. His conscience gave him no rest, and no one believed that he was innocent. He became one of the heaviest drinkers that I ever saw."

---

[74] Davis was a carpenter at Palmer and Jones' whaling station. Palmer allegedly tried to bribe Davis to stay silent.

[75] The Preservation Inlet Manslaughter Trial, 1838. Palmer was tried and found not guilty at the Supreme Criminal Court in Sydney on Wednesday, May 16, 1838. The trial proceedings were not published in New Zealand. The proceedings are available in McNab 1913:204-220.

[76] Many of Palmers' 'witnesses' testified that Denahan was sickly with worms from eating muttonfish (paua) prior to the beating.

[77] It was John Jones that intimated he wanted Davis up for perjury.

"Well he was a brute anyway,' said Jack, vehemently, 'but tell us more about Old Jock, Grandfather."

"Very well," said Grandfather, "I'll tell you about the time we were together in Breaksea Sound. We were sperm whaling there and did very well too, getting about 18 or 19 tuns of oil. That at about £100 per tun wasn't bad for a few months work was it? We were waiting for the *Kariri* to come down, and we ran out of food. Sometimes we managed to knock down a bird, and we could get fish and pawa.

We also had a thin biscuit made of water and flour every day. Jock would never eat his, thought the rest of us ate ours greedily enough. He always gave his to a half-caste boy named Kundi Graham, of whom he was very fond. Kundi used to beg him to eat it himself, but Jock would say, 'Tut, tut boy, I wouldn't dirty my mouth with it. You need it, and I don't.'

He never seemed to mind going without food, though he could eat sometimes. He used to tell with great gusto how he 'had' Mrs Guard[78] once. He was lightering on the river for Jack Guard, and one day he and another chap came in about two o'clock. The rest had all finished dinner. Mrs Guard was a very mean woman, but she had to give them their meals, so she brought out with no very good grace a joint of meat she had cooked for supper, and cut them each a very little for two hungry men. So they asked for more, and again she served them in the same way. A third time they passed up their plates, and once more she gave them the same meagre supply. The fourth time, however she became angry, and pushing the joint to Jock, told him he had better eat it all, never dreaming for a moment that he would. She then left the room, and Jock and his mate went steadily on, and when Mrs Guard came in again, Jock was picking at the bone!

Jock used to say that when she saw him, her face was a study, and the poor old man would laugh till he cried when he told us about it.

---

[78] Betty Guard (nee Parker) married John "Jacky" Guard in 1830. Betty was 15, Jack was nearly 40. Betty was one of the first European women to settle in southern New Zealand and, although probably in her teens during the story above, was renowned as being as tough as her husband.

Jock was married to a Maori woman by Bishop Selwyn, but his wife did not live long. He was such a nice old fellow. Everyone liked old Jock – from the oldest man to the youngest child. He came up to see me in '70 'for the last time,' he said. I couldn't bear saying good-bye to the dear old chap. I can see him now, with tears running down his old face, and saying how he would have liked to have seen all the children together again. But bless you, they were all over the place. Very soon after Jock went back to Fortrose he died. He was a very old man, though I don't know his exact age. He was as true a friend as man could have, and numbers, both old and young, mourned sincerely for old Jock. I have a photograph of him which I will show you if you like, if Fred will bring me my desk.

Elizabeth 'Betty' Guard silhouette, c.1830s. Courtesy of the Guard family.

# Chapter 11

## *CHASLAND'S MISTAKE – HOW IT WAS NAMED –*
## *EYES LIKE A HAWK – THE ACHERON IN BLIGH SOUND –*
## *GOVERNOR GREY AT PORT CHALMERS*

"Grandfather, don't you think that Chasland's Mistake is a queer name to give a place?" asked Fred looking up from his atlas.

"No, I think it's a very appropriate name," said Grandfather, "and if you come here I'll tell you how it came to be called so.

One day Chasland and some other men were coming along in his boat, when he saw what Chasland himself called 'a power of seals' on the headland. But they had no salt with them, so they came down as fast as they could to Port William, where Tommy had left his salt.

When they got to Port William they were very mysterious, and would not say a word as to where they were going, for they thought they were going to do a big stroke. But when they got back to the place where they had seen the seals, there was not one to be found. By degrees the story leaked out, but it wasn't wise to say 'seal' to Tommy for some time after that. So perhaps the name doesn't seem so queer to you now Fred, that you see where the mistake comes in. He should have killed the seals while he was sure of them, but he was afraid the skins would not keep till he got the skins down to the salt, for seal skins are not like other skins, having a good deal of fat about them, and the weather was not good enough to risk drying them[79].

Tommy was a Sydney half-caste, and like most of his race had wonderful eyesight. Talk about a hawk. No hawk that ever flew had keener eyes than Tommy.  Once he was out sealing in the *Glory* brig with a Captain Swindles,

---

[79] Another version suggests that Chasland 'mistook' the land for the Otago Heads.

and they were wrecked on the Chatham Islands[80]. They had a boat and Chasland declared that he would come to N.Z. in it. It was a small open boat named the Paramatta; and of course they ran a great risk in going that distance.

However Captain Anglem and Captain Swindles agreed to go with him. Tommy's Maori wife, Poona, was with him and he tried to persuade her to stay with the others until next sealing season, when he would come back for them. She wouldn't say whether she'd stay or not, but when they launched the boat, and were just setting off she ran out into the water after them, up to her waist, and they had to take her. That woman was very fond of Tommy, and no mistake, he was just as fond of her. He was a grand old chap too, but a terror to drink.

Tommy steered all the way from Chatham Islands till they were quite close to N.Z. and one fine morning when there was very little wind, but rather a heavy sea running. Captain Swindles offered to steer so that Tommy could have a sleep.

---

[80] The *Glory* wrecked on Pitt's Island/Rangiauria (the second largest island in the Chatham Islands) in early 1827. The area is now known as Glory Bay. Once they reached New Zealand and rescued the crew, Swindells and some of the crew (minus Anglem and Chasland) departed for Sydney aboard the *Samuel*, arriving April 1827. The official report in the *Australian* (Tuesday 20 March 1827) stated:

> *We regret to state the total loss of the brig Glory, belonging to this port, on the 10th of January last. The circumstance occurred whilst the Glory was laying to an anchor at Pitt's Island, in lat. 44.25. At eight o'clock she struck the ground. A stream anchor was carried out, and efforts used to rope off the vessel, but in vain, though a heavy ground swell continue to urge her on to certain destruction. After striking again so forcibly as to shake her frame nearly asunder, Captain Swindells succeeded in running her ashore on the beach, and saving the sails and rigging, which, with her provisions, eight hundred skins, six or eight tons of flax, and a quantity of pork in casks,- have been rescued from destruction. Fortunately not a single life was lost. The long boat was got on shore, pitched, painted, and being provided with wash-boards, masts, sails, and a sufficiency of provisions, Captain Swindells and five men steered their course in her for New Zealand, a distance of eight hundred miles, and were (fortunate enough to reach the entrance to the Bay of Islands, at the critical moment of the schooner Samuel coming out. Captain. S. and his adventurous boat's crew, have reached Sydney in safety.' — Mr. R. Campbell, Jun. and Mr. Emmett, have each one quarter share in the cargo, and Captain Swindells one half. They have been singularly fortunate — the hull of the brig being insured at £100. None of the property that was not insured has been lost or injured in any way.*

So Chasland gave him the tiller; but he hadn't had it a minute before he let a big sea come right over the boat, so Tommy got up again and never let go of the tiller till they were safely landed at Moeraki.

But they were anxious to get down to the Straits to catch a sealing vessel that would take them back to Sydney; and so Tommy climbed a hill to see if he could see any sign of a ship about. While he was up there he happened to glance at the little Maori house they were living in, which was more than a mile away, and through the tiny window he saw Captain Swindles trying to kiss Poona. Chasland ran as hard as he could down to the captain and, to use his own language, 'slapped his jaws for him.' He was awfully anxious to leave Swindles there, but Captain Anglem begged him to take the fellow with them. Tommy did it, but oh he was wild!

Afterwards Tommy Chasland went round in the *Acheron* with Captain Stokes, Marine Surveyor. One night they were going up Bligh's Sound. Chasland was taking her up, and the captain was on the bridge with his night glass.

'We'll have to stop now, sir, and let down the anchor,' Tommy said

'Oh no Chasland, we're not near shore yet,' said the captain.

'I tell you, if she paddles another stroke we'll be ashore,' said Chasland, 'can't you see that tree on the flat?'

But the captain could see nothing and would not give the order to stop, and in half a minute they had touched the bottom; so they had to back her off and anchor. All the midshipmen were up at daylight to see if there was any tree, as Chasland had said, and there, sure enough, was a tree standing alone on the flat.

But really his eyesight was wonderful. Once he and another Sydney black named Malby were on Codfish, and the people there were in a great state because a son of the Wakataupuka (Bloody Jack's cousin) had died there, and they were afraid that the Maori's would kill some of them as a kind of sacrifice – as was their custom when anyone of note died. They were all keeping a look out, expecting every day to see the Maori's coming.

One day Chasland said he could see them coming in canoes through a passage at Raggity[81]. He and Malby counted them at that distance – about five miles off.

'There are eleven, Tommy,' said Malby.

'You are a liar,' said Tommy 'there are only ten.'

Malby told him to look behind the fourth canoe and he'd see a small one, and so he did. On came the canoes and when they were close to the beach the people sent Tommy Topi – a young chief – to tell them not to land, as Codfish people were armed and ready to fight.

'What do they want to fight for?' inquired the Wakataupuka.

'Oh,' said Topi, 'they think you are going to kill some of them because of your son's death here.'

'I'm not going to harm anyone,' said the chief. 'He would have died all the same if he'd been with me. We have come to have a tangi[82] over him.'

And what a feast and jollification they did have to be sure. No one would imagine anyone had died. Of course those related to the dead did not join in the general carousing. They supplied the food and all their neighbours ate till they couldn't see, while the bereaved ones mourned and fasted for a certain time.

When the first man-of-war came to Otago, Governor Grey was aboard. She was lying outside and a number of the boats went out to her, and the men went aboard. The captain was on the bridge and he called out:

'Is there a man there that will pilot her Britannic Majesty's ship into Port Chalmers?' Not a voice answered though there were two captains on board that had been used to going in and out.

---

[81] Rugged Islands, to the north east of Codfish Island.

[82] Tangi - mourning ceremony

Tommy Chasland waited for a minute, and as there was no response to the captain's offer of £20 or £30 (I don't know exactly how much).

'By the hole of my coat, sir, I'll take her in for you,' said Tommy.

'Come up then my man,' said the captain with a laugh, and up Tommy went and took the vessel into Port Chalmers. They offered him the position of pilot there, but he would not take it on the plea of being too old; but he really knew that he wasn't to be trusted, as whenever he had money he got drunk."

Governor Grey, c.1860.

# Chapter 12

*A CHAPTER OF MAORI HISTORY – A TERRIBLE REVENGE*

"Grandfather, you promised to tell us about some of the West Coast caves tonight," said Fred.

"So I did," said Grandfather, "but I was just thinking about a notorious old chief, so I'll tell you about him instead, if you don't mind, and we will leave the cave till another time."

We all said we did not mind and gathered round to hear the yarn.

"Well the Mahurunui[83] was a bloodthirsty old villain, and no mistake," began Grandfather.

"What did he do?" asked Fred.

"Do? Why he murdered numbers of innocent people for no good cause whatsoever, and ate any amount too. It's a good thing he never saw you Fred. You'd have just been a good breakfast for him… It would make your hair stand on end to hear some of the things the Maoris tell about the Mahurunui, but I was thinking about his death, of which I'll tell you.

He lived at Akaroa[84]. He was very high in rank, and had great authority over the other tribes. He heard that some of the North Island Maoris were coming down to Kaiapoi to get greenstone, so over he went and told the people there that when the Maoris came they were to kill them, for if they didn't, the North Islanders would go back to their homes and come again and kill THEM, and take

---

[83] Te Maiharanui/Tamaiharanui, Ngāti Rakiamoa (b. late 1700's - d.1830/31), the paramount chief of the Akaroa area. Te Maiharanui was also a central figure in the intertribal Kai Huanga (eat relations) feud (c.1826).

[84] Takapuneke village (Red House Bay near Akaroa).

possession of the place. So at last he over-persuaded the people, and when the unsuspecting natives came the Southern Maoris overpowered and killed them all. There were three chiefs and all their men[85].

When the news reached the North Island, the natives rested neither day nor night till they got their revenge. They made several fruitless attempts to capture the Mahurunui.

One day a brig went to Kapiti (where the massacred people came from) to buy potatoes. I think the name of the brig was the *Elizabeth*, but I'm not certain.

The head chief and his men boarded the brig, and informed the captain that they were going to take the vessel; but that they would not harm any of them nor take their things. All that they wanted was that the captain should take them down to Akaroa and bring them back again.

So what could the poor captain do – if he hadn't taken them he'd have been killed, and all his crew, but I believe he got into hot water over it afterwards[86]. They arrived at Akaroa one beautiful afternoon[87], and going up the harbour all the Maoris went below, knowing that the Mahurunui would see the brig and come aboard, thinking to trade.

Presently the chief came alongside in the royal canoe with a good number of men and his daughter. They all quickly boarded the vessel. No sooner did the last man step on board, when up rushed the Maoris from below, and Mahurunui and all his crew were taken prisoners – all except one man. He would have been no better than the rest, only the cook kept making signs to him, indicating danger of some kind or another, and pointing down below, and there he saw some Maoris preparing to rush up the ladder to seize them.

---

[85] Probably in 1829

[86] Captain John Stewart of the *Elizabeth* allegedly entered into a commercial relationship with Te Rauparaha to transport the war party. Stewart went to court in Sydney but due to lack of "reliable" (aka Pakeha) evidence he was released.

[87] 11 November 1830

Quick as thought he jumped overboard, and while the tussle was going on in the ship he managed to swim ashore unharmed. He then warned the others and those that were able fled. The ones that were not overtaken and killed eventually made their way to Nelson.

With Maoris, as with most others, in a case of imminent danger, self was uppermost, and many strong and stalwart men fled, leaving their aged mothers, crippled fathers and helpless children to the mercy of a tribe mad with hatred and burning with vengeance.

Of course there were a few beautiful and noble exceptions, where heroic fathers, sons and husbands stayed behind to aid the weaker ones, but only at the cost of their lives. On came the pursuers and those of the retreating party who were overtaken were butchered with disgusting brutality.

After they had slain all but a few whom they took as slaves, the North Islanders again joined the brig and set off home in high spirits, having obtained their heart's desire. Revenge to them was sweet indeed.

The captain obtained permission for the Mahurunui's daughter to come up on deck, and one day when the brig was scudding rapidly along, she watched her chance, this Maori princess, and jumped overboard and was drowned at once. It was better thus for her, as she would have been tortured to death otherwise.

The death they gave her father was the most dreadful they could devise… they crucified him – nailed him to a tree, and then the outraged wives and mothers of the chiefs he had murdered without a cause, prodded him to death with red-hot iron gun ramrods, telling him all the time what it was for and why they were doing it.

It was a slow and most agonising death, but he bore it without a murmur. It is dreadful to think that women could do such a thing, but as they were only ruled by their fierce ungoverned passions, it seemed to them the right thing to do[88]."

---

[88] Stack recounts a variation of this story in Jacobson's 'Tales of Banks Peninsula' (1914) see next page:

Te Rauparaha. After Charles Heaphy. 1839.

"*Captain Stewart sent repeated messages to [Maiharanui] to hasten his coming [to the ship], and on the eighth day he arrived, accompanied by his wife, Te Whe, and his little daughter, Nga roi mata. He was cordially welcomed on reaching the deck by the captain, who took him below to the cabin. He was hardly seated before a door opened, and Te Rauparaha entered, accompanied by several of his companions, who at once seized Te Maiharanui, and taunted him with his simplicity in permitting himself to be so readily entrapped.*"

He goes on to describe the pillaging of the settlement:

"*One the second day after Te Maiharanui's capture, Te Rauparaha attacked Takapuneke very early in the morning. The place was unfortified and undefended. About one hundred persons were killed, and fifty were taken on board as prisoners. After the destruction of the kainga, the vessel sailed away to Kapiti.*"

Stack then suggests a different fate for Te Maiharanui's daughter:

"*Te Maiharanui smothered his little daughter, Nga roi mata, appropriately named 'The Tears' less she should become the wife of one of his enemies.*

The Stack description of the torture of Te Maiharanui is identical to the narrators account.

# Chapter 13

*THE WEST COAST CAVES – A PETRIFIED MAN – OLD-TIME MEMORIES*

*CAPTAIN HOWELL – JACK PRICE AND HIS WAYS*

"You'll tell us about the West Coast[89] caves tonight, won't you Grandfather?" said Fred

"Very well my boy. There are some splendid caves round there. In '35 I think it was, we went into Breaksea Sound in the schooner *Amazon*. It was a rough night and looked very wild. We went some distance and Captain Howell told me to sound. I found that close to the rocks there were 18 fathoms of water; but the wind sprang up in the night and blew frightfully. In the morning it lulled and we went four of five miles further up the sound and anchored in nine fathoms of water, with a muddy bottom.

We found a cave there recently vacated by the Maoris. They must have heard us the previous night and ran off and left everything. We could see where the women had been making their mats. They left hem all – some half finished, others just begun.

There was a beautifully carved battleaxe too, made from the jawbone of a sperm whale. It was a grand cave. All the Maoris belonging to our boat used to sleep there. They called it Hawea's cave, declaring that a chief of that name, who lived in the bush used to sleep there. [90]

---

[89] South-west Fiordland

There are lots of caves in Chalky[91] but there was one tremendous one called Morgan's cave. Morgan was a Welshman and he and his boat's crew made a home in this cave. It was divided into a number of rooms with ferntrees and they made it altogether comfortable, but I believe it's fallen in now. The rock was certainly very soft. There are plenty of smaller caves there though, and quite safe too. I slept in them many a night.

On the left hand side going up Preservation towards 'Old Billy's' are some limestone caves. They are not very easy to find. We were whaling there for years and never saw them. The land is wooded to the water's edge, and though we passed close by in a boat hundreds of times, we never saw the caves until and old chap showed them to us.

Some men used to make a good deal of money gathering the guano from the caves in Preservation, and they got to know the coast there pretty well. One day they found a new cave, and on going in, the first thing that struck their eye was a man's figure standing upright. They were terribly frightened and went out quicker than they went in; but after a while some of the bolder ones ventured in again, and found that it was a man's perfect form turned into stone. Every feature, even the hair, was quite distinct.

---

[90] The Hawea hapu (clan) of the Kati Mamoe tribe are sometime referred to as the "lost tribe" of Maori legend. Their final pa (fortified village) in Fiordland was Matauira Pa on Spit Island, Preservation Inlet. It resisted an assault by Ngai Tahu in the late 1700's but fell to a cunning second attack where famed Ngai Tahu Chief, Maru, acted as a seal in front of the pa, thus luring the Hawea tribe out of their fort unarmed except with seal clubs. Many were killed but a few were away on a hunting expedition. When they saw the fate of their village they reputedly disappeared off into the wilds of Fiordland. On March 26, 1773 Captain Cook noted the presence of three or four native families believed to be the remnants of the tribe living in Dusky Sound. John Hall-Jones recounts a similar tale in the Fjords of Fiordland (p.83), except that it was in 1842 when Paddy Gilroy then captain of the *Amazon*, sailed into Bligh Sound (about 100 km north of Breaksea) looking for seals. He saw smoke coming from a cave and the crew landed to find sleeping and cooking quarters, as well as fishing baskets, mats and a whalebone mere. The Maori crew chased the fugitives up the mountain but never caught up with them. Gilroy took away the mat (see picture in Beattie *Maoris of Fiordland* 1949) and mere.

[91] The Preservation and Chalky Inlet areas are honeycombed with caves. Archaeologists have proven that Maori, sealers and whalers utilised them for temporary shelters (Coutts 1969, Smith 2002).

They supposed that the man died in the cave and the drippings from the limestone above in a short time petrified him. The men wanted to get the stone man out and bring it round here, but some sailors who were there at the time got into the cave and broke up the body and knocked off the head, so they thought it was no use to bring in pieces.

There's a splendid cave at Price's. It's easy to find, though I knew some chaps who whaled there for two seasons and never saw a sign of it. There are two entrances to Price's cave – one in the bush and open opening on the beach. Jack Price lived there with all his boat's crew. He used to block up one entrance – the back door he used to call it – because the wind blew right through the cave sometimes.

The Maoris would not believe that Jack Price was an ordinary man. They called him Tumuraki[92], which means some relation to the devil. He used to go out in such awful weather, and yet he'd be whistling and singing, let it blow ever so hard, and he'd do things in a boat that no one else ever dared to do, and yet nothing ever happened to him. One day there were four boats round at The Looking Glass, as we used to call a fall round there, which, at a distance, looked exactly like a long mirror. They came on in a tremendous rookery of seals, but the weather was so bad they decided to wait for a better day. Jack Price had left his salt down at the cave, and though it was fearfully rough he persuaded the men to go with him for it. They got down that day for it, and the next he wanted to start back to the seals, but the wind changed south and the men all said there was too much sea on to go back at once.

So Price said to them that they'd go as far as Preservation and catch some fish, and then if it was still rough they would go up the Sound. When they had caught the fish it was as rough, or rougher, than ever; but Price was up sail, and took two reefs in the lug, and then headed the boat for the West coast before any of the men dreamt of his intention.

---

[92] A variation of Tumuraki, Raki-tumu, means "threatening sky" and was, perhaps coincidentally, one of the Maori names for Preservation Inlet. J Hall-Jones Fiords of Fiordland p.89 and Otago Witness 10 November 1909, p.13.

They had to make the best of it however, and they got round all right. Price hauled his boat right up in the rookery of seals, and killed every one, getting as many as 300 skins. Two days later, when the weather got finer, the three other boats came for their share. What was their disgust and surprise to find no seals, and Price's skins all salted and spread about the rocks.

Tommy Chasland was dreadfully angry about it. To think that they had wasted several days waiting for fine weather and Price had stolen such a march on them when they thought he hadn't come back from Preservation!

Jack Price died in the cave. One day they had a tremendous run round the coast, and Price said he was tired, and went to bed early. He had some funny ways. For instance, he always carried the plug of the boat with him. This night, after he had been in bed some time, he raised himself on his elbow and called to the others, who were sitting round the fire. He gave the plug to Long Harry, saying he didn't think he'd ever use it again. And before morning he was dead.

He never used a rudder, and it is heavy work steering with an oar always, and they thought he overdid it. He was a splendid boatman, I've heard many a man say. They buried him up in the bush, and Long Harry carved his name, age, and date of his birth on a piece of an old canoe. I've often seen the grave. The trees were a tremendous height around it, and it looked very dark and gloomy.

# Chapter 14

*THE WEST COAST CAVES – A NARROW ESCAPE –*

*GEORGE PAULEY AND THE CZAR'S DAUGHTER*

"Anymore yarns about the West Coast caves, Grandfather?" asked Jack.

"Oh there are numbers of caves there that I never saw boy, but there are a good many on Crayfish Island we used to go into. They run in a long way too, and there are any amount of human bones in them. There's one at the back of the old fishery that we could never reach the end of.

One year a lot of Maoris and white people were mutton-birding on Kundy's Island[93]. The Maoris slept in whares[94] up the hill, but the white people slept in a cave on the beach. It came on very bad weather, and the cave was leaking and dripping, making everything uncomfortable. One man named George Parker built himself a hut, and then sold it to another man for four pieces of tobacco, and built himself another. Then they all built little huts for themselves; and the very day after the last man moved out of the cave, it fell in. There was a landslip caused by the constant rain.

Brown had a new boat, of which he was very proud, and all the boats were hauled up to the mouth of the cave. The very morning the cave fell in, Brown asked old Bob Watson to go and see if the boats were all right.

'They're alright,' said Watson, 'every nail is an anchor now.'

Everybody ran down to the shore to see what he meant, and there they saw the slip. The falling earth had filled and sunk several of the boats, and a great stone weighing several tons had rolled into Brown's boat, and then bounded into the next boat, the *Moko*, belonging to George Pauley.

---

[93] Kundy Island is a 19 hectare island about 6km north of Easy Harbour, Stewart Island.

[94] *Whares* = houses

Brown's boat was not damaged nearly so much as the *Moko*, but he followed the Maori fashion and smashed it to pieces, refusing offers of £10 to £20, which were made. The Maoris had a great dislike of mending things, and there was no very good carpenter there at the time. It was a ridiculous and extravagant fashion, though, they had of destroying things.

The *Moko* was patched up pretty well, and they took her to Preservation to paint her. She was painted and left in a large cave there which bears its name, but she wouldn't dry in the cave and had to be brought out again.

Of all the comical men I ever met, I think George Pauley was the most comical. He used to keep us amused by the hour. He went round Australia and through Torres Strait with Captain King in a revenue cutter, the first time that voyage was ever made. When they entered Sydney Harbour on their return they were firing a salute, and Pauley somehow lost some fingers off his right hand in touching one of the guns.

Pauley was very well read and had a splendid memory. He could remember perfectly all he read and all he heard. He would describe rocks and trees, places and people and things with such accuracy that even those who were quite familiar with what he was talking about would not believe that he was not speaking of what he had seen.

If the sailors spoke of any place they had been, he'd tell them that he'd been there, and tell them even more about the place than they knew themselves. If the rest of us told them that in reality Pauley had never been out of the colonies they would not believe us.

But it was the fun of the world to hear him talking to a stranger. We used to sit and listen, alternately marvelling and half-choking in our efforts to keep from laughing aloud.

He'd tell them that he came out from England as a great botanist, that he went through all his fortune, but that he hoped in time to be reinstated. He always spoke so seriously and with such conviction that very few disbelieved him.

He used to say too, that when in Russia the Czar's daughter fell so desperately in love with him that he was in a very embarrassing position.

'She used to bother me so and write to me so often,' Pauley would say, 'that at last I had to give her a plump denial.'

That yarn always finished us, and we used to roar at him, but he was never disconcerted a whit. Poor old Pauley! One thing is certain: his romancing never did anyone the least harm, although it often amused a good many of us. He never turned his 'gift of the gab' as the sailors called it, to evil account.

Now boys, that will do for tonight. It's time you were all in bed, and I'm tired too."

Captain King's sketch of the *Mermaid* at Oyster Bay, 1818.

# Chapter 15

*NED THE ROVER – A PERILOUS DIVE – CAPTAIN ANGLEM –*

*HIS EARLY CAREER SEARCHING FOR GREENSTONE –*

*A VALUABLE FIND*

"There's another cave round the west side that I forgot to tell you about," said Grandfather, "it's in Dusky Bay. There's only a small opening above water, just large enough to pass things through. It's on the side of a perpendicular cliff, and under the water there's a large opening in to the cave beyond.

One day a lot of fellows were round there and on looking through the top hole of the rocks they saw about a dozen seals in the water inside the cave. They had a little chap with them whom we called Ned the Rover, and they made him believe that good divers often dived into this cave to get the seals; so after a while down he went. He got in alright, and they handed him a torch and a gun through the upper opening.

He fastened the torch in the rocks and shot 10 or 11 seals and passed the skins out to the others. Then he attempted to come out again, but somehow he missed the passage and by the time he came up again in the cave, blood was gushing from his mouth, ears and nose.

He waited long enough to recover himself and then tried again, and this time he was successful. The other men were frightened that he was drowned and sorry that they had made him go, and they were very much relieved when he made his appearance.

Nobody was ever in Ned the Rover's Cave either before or since, as far as I know. I never heard what Ned's name was. The first time I ever saw him was early in the year 1835.    We were coming to New Zealand in the *Lucy Ann* when one afternoon we were just off Howe's Island[95] and Captain Anglem told me to take a boat ashore and get some fish.

So Bosun, Black Dick, and I lowered a boat and commenced pulling to the shore. We thought then that Howe's Island was uninhabited, but before we reached it we met a boat coming out to sea.

There were two men and their wives and a Maori boy in it. One of the men asked the names of the ship and captain. When I told him, he said he knew Captain Anglem and they all came to N.Z. with us. Ned had a very nice garden on the island with pumpkins, melons, and I don't know what all in it. Both the men, I think had escaped from Sydney in a whaler, and had been landed on Howe's Island; but they had not been long there when we took them off. Ned was a very decent little fellow."

"Grandfather, I wish you'd tell us something more about Captain Anglem," said Jack, "I think he's a grand sort."

"Very well, I'll tell you all I know," said Grandfather, "he's often told me about his life. I don't ever remember hearing him speak of his parents, but when quite a child he was placed in a monastery to be educated as a priest. He received an excellent education and was a good linguist, and he could speak several languages fluently. At one time he was very devout, and he and a young medical student, a college classmate, made a pilgrimage to the tomb of some saint. They were humiliating themselves as much as possible in the presence of the holy bones, when the student noticed that the bones did not all belong to the same skeleton; that in fact, there were some missing, and there were more than the right numbers of others. They were both right awfully disgusted.

Captain Anglem found out that he had no 'vocation' for a priest and ran away to sea, and came out to Hobart in the *Lady Castle Forbes*. He then fell in with a very rich man called Lone, and he was with him for a long time. Lone had been a large sugar merchant on the Isle of France, but he left it when the English took possession there, and he came to Hobart with his wife, mother-in-law, his little

---

[95] Lord Howe's Island, Great Barrier Reef, 500 km east of Sydney.

daughter, and a crowd of French servants.

My sister and I often went to play with Laura Lone, and it was there I first saw Anglem, though I didn't recognise him again when I saw him in Otago. He then went to Sydney with Mr Lone, and when the latter went to Ireland, Anglem went sealing in several different vessels. I told you about his being cast away in the *Glory*.

He was on a boat called the *Royal Mail*, taking greenstone from N.Z. to Manilla[96]. They made a tremendous profit out of the greenstone. It was made into crucifixes and images, and sold very well. At first they couldn't find the greenstone, so Captain Anglem came to Bluff and got a very old Maori who had travelled a great deal on the West Coast, to go with him and point out the greenstone which they could not distinguish from the other rocks. The Maori knew where it was perfectly well, but he pretended that he didn't and went off into a deep sleep, as he called it, and when he awoke he took them straight to the spot.

It was a tremendous rock, and the next difficulty was to break it up. They could not manage it for a long time, but at last a man came and drilled holes in it, and they blasted it with powder, and had several accidents. Captain Anglem lost an eye, and so did an old Rivertonian named Bates[97], it was rather difficult to lay a train of powder, and of course they had no fuse.

Captain King of the *Arnetta*, was an awfully jolly young fellow. We all liked him immensely. I don't know what became of him afterwards. They tried to keep it quiet where they were getting the greenstone from, in case anybody else would try to get some too.

One day Tommy Chasland was on a reef at Cascade Point and about 18 or 19 miles off he espied a ship sailing into Martin's Bay, so he ordered his men to row him there at once. They didn't believe he saw a boat, and didn't want to go, but they had to. When they got near enough, Chasland said to the rowers:

---

[96] Anglem also took greenstone to China in the early 1840s. Howard 1939:91-2.

[97] Nathaniel Bates.

'Now turn round, and you will see their things hanging on the bushes.'

And sure enough they did – blankets and clothes, and the like, but before they could land, those on shore had seen them and quickly hid all their things and themselves too; but Tommy shouted out to show themselves or he'd pretty quickly find them, so they came out. They were the men left behind to blast the rock and pack it in boxes made on purpose so that the sailors couldn't steal the stone. Tommy satisfied his curiosity and went back to his own work. I will tell you about Captain Anglem some other time."

# Chapter 16

*AT SEA WITH CAPTAIN ANGLEM – A BORN NAVIGATOR –*

*SOME OF HIS WAYS - A GOOD MAN AND TRUE.*

"Grandfather," we all begged, "do go on with the story about Captain Anglem."

"All right boys, I'll tell you about the first voyage I ever went with him.

It was in 1835. We left Sydney in the *Lucy Ann* to go sperm whaling. The weather was very rough, and we only got two whales all the season. We had been in a terrible gale for over a week. I was sure we were 40 or 50 miles from the land. The captain hadn't taken sun for five or six days and the only thing we had was a 'tell-tale' compass which hung in the cabin and that is all the captain went by.

One night, just after I had given the men their 8 o'clock grog, the captain said to me. 'Whose is the morning watch?'

'Mine sir,' I answered.

'Well, call me when you get up will you?'

And so I did. He told me to go on deck and see if the weather was as rough as ever. I went up and all the watch were standing by the companion. Some of them said the weather was worse, and some said it was better. I went below and told Captain Anglem that I didn't think it blew so hard. He said,

'Give the watch a glass of grog; veer the ship round, loose the foretopsail, and shake the reef out of the main-topsail.'

When I went up and told the watch they all declared he was drunk, and some of them went for'ard and told the others, and soon there wasn't a man below but the captain himself.

When I took the empty bottle back I asked the Captain how far we were from land.

'This morning at 8 o'clock we'll be between Codfish Island and the Solanders.' he said.

I went up on deck and told the men. They all swore he was mad. It was enough to make them think so too, when they thought they were hundreds of miles from land. It was blowing and raining frightfully. The white water was flying and such a sea on too; but the brave little *Lucy Ann* sailed like a duck and never took a drop except rain water.

We had two Australian natives with us, and Black Dick was particularly fond of rum, so I told him that if he'd keep a good look-out I'd give him a bottle of rum. He climbed up the foreyard and sat in the lea of the mast, and long before daylight he called out 'Land-ho!'

'Where away, Dick?' asked the captain, who heard from the cabin.

'A little on the lea bow, sir.'

'That's Codfish, Dick. Now look to wind'ard and you'll see Solanders.' And it was a long time before any of us, except Black Bosun could see Codfish. When the sun came up we were just off Smoky Cove, on the N.W. of Stewart Island. Then it was laughable how all the men changed their tune. An hour and a half before they hadn't the language bad enough to express their opinions of Captain Anglem, and now they were able to go round the world with him!

But he was a very clever fellow, make no mistake. Once he was up at Port Nicholson, and there he met a certain Colonel Godfrey, and they became very friendly, as countrymen in the same station of life are apt to do. When Captain Anglem came back to Stewart Island, where he was living then at the Old Neck, he sent Colonel Godfrey some charts he had made of the East Coast of the South Island and most of the coast of Stewart Island.

Colonel Godfrey gave these charts to Captain Stokes[98] when he came down here. Anglem, poor fellow, was dead then. Captain Stokes asked me what instruments Anglem had when he made the sketches. When I told him that Anglem had nothing but a common quadrant, he would hardly believe me.

'He must have been an uncommonly clever man,' said Captain Stokes, 'my midshipmen and I took all the bearings and there isn't the faintest mistake anywhere in Anglem's work, and he had to take the stars too, to find the longitude. He's a born navigator. I would have liked to have known him.'

Carter and I were the only ones with Captain Anglem when he died. One afternoon a Maori came with the news that the captain was ill, so Carter and I went to him at once. We arrived just at dusk and found him in violent convulsions. It was all that we could do to hold him, and this continued at intervals all through the night, till just at dawn he died. He wasn't conscious for a moment all the time.

He was as nice a fellow as one could wish to meet, always polite and gentlemanly, and what was rather exceptional in those days, he was never known to swear. In height he was about 5ft 10in, very fair and clear complexioned, and on the whole very nice-looking. He was witty and smart in lots of ways, especially in making fun of people and taking rises out of them, but like a good many people though he could make a joke, he couldn't take one, and I remember he was very angry because he met his match in Captain King.

Captain Anglem had a great trick of picking up the newspaper or a book and pretending to read out of it, when in reality he was only making up what he said as he went along, and he turned out such witty and also such connected articles that he often took us all in. One night we were all sitting round the fire and Captain Anglem produced a newspaper from his pocket and offered to read. The offer was accepted with delight, for newspapers were not plentiful in those days.

---

[98] Captain John Lort Stokes, skipper of the *Acheron* (b.1811 – d.1885). The *Acheron* was a paddle steamer survey ship that produced the first accurate charts of Foveaux Strait and Fiordland in 1849.

He read for a time all right and then he said something about the population of N.Z. being made up of two-thirds of absentees and runaway prisoners from Hobart and Sydney, hitting at two or three in the company present. But one old man cried out:

'Oh yes, I read that. The other third is made up of broken down captains!' and even Anglem couldn't help but join in the laugh raised against himself.

But he was a thorough gentleman and a true friend, Captain Anglem, and all that knew him liked and respected him."

Captain John Lort Stokes, 1864. After William Egley.

# Chapter 17

## *A BLANKET FOR A DOG – A CUTE TRICK STEALING A HEAD*

"Now boys," said Grandfather, "if you want a yarn tonight, I'll tell you about the Wakataupuka, Bloody Jacks cousin[99].

I think I told you before about the first night we ran away from the ship – how the Wakataupuka gave us protection. Well, a little after that, one nasty drizzling day, I'd just come off the stage and had the spade still in my hand when one of the men said to me, 'You can't hit that dog.' Pointing to a little terrier not many yards away.

Without a moment's thought I let the spade fly and it just glanced over the dogs back, and off it went howling. It went so quickly that we couldn't see whether I'd done any damage or not.

But next morning, just as we were launching the boat, down came Taiaroa, and didn't he talk to me! But I couldn't understand a word he said till a man who had been sometime in N.Z. came and interpreted for me.

Then I understood that I had killed Taiaroa's dog and he wanted payment for it. The man who was telling me what Taiaroa said advised me to settle with him at once. 'If you don't,' he said, 'as soon as the boats go he'll go and take everything in the house.'

So I said, 'Ask him what he wants then.' So he asked him and Taiaroa said he would like a blanket.

I had to go up to Mr Weller's and get him a blanket. Mr Weller told me I was very foolish to kill the man's dog. Dogs were scarce in those days and the Maoris set great store on them.

---

[99] Some whakapapa (genealogies) record Whakataupuka as Tuhawaiki/Bloody Jack's uncle.

'Besides,' said Mr Weller, 'if you enrage the Maoris they might massacre us all, and we stand no chance against them. It's best to keep friendly with them.[100]

So I gave Taiaroa the blanket with many apologies and I had almost forgotten the circumstances when, four or five months later, the Wakataupuka came to Otago. One morning he came up to me and said,

'You kill Taiaroa's dog?' I thought he wanted another payment, but I said:

'Yes, I killed it.'

'No,' he said, 'kuri[101] all right – kuri not dead.' I stared at him. He laughed and said, 'Come alonga me.' So I went with him through the bush to Taiaroa's house.

The first little dog that ran out barking at us was the one I was supposed to have killed. I didn't recognise the dog, but the Wakataupuka knew it. He took me inside and Mrs Taiaroa was the only one at home. He ordered the woman to give me back my blanket. It took her quite half an hour to find it. She hunted through dozens of baskets, and the things she had astonished me, and at last from out of her spoils she drew my blanket. When I went back to the white's settlement with my blanket over my arm Jack Hughes said to me, 'My word! You are a favourite.'[102]

At the end of that season, a ship called the *John Barry* came in to take oil to Sydney. Her captain heard from Mr Weller that the Maoris at Old Taitoo's kaik[103] had a Maori man's head preserved, and he offered the Wakataupuka £5 for it.

---

[100] The previous year there were reports of hostilities between the local Maori and Weller's whaling station (Sydney Herald September 28, 1834). To contextualise the aggression, southern Maori had only just come back from a raid against Te Rauparaha at Cloudy Bay where their enemy had eluded them. In frustration they struck out at both local Maori and whalers. The following year, when this story takes place, Maori-Pakeha relations had vastly improved.

[101] *Kuri* - dog

[102] A variation of the story of William Thomas, Taiaroa and Whakataupuka was recounted in the Otago Witness (17 May 1905). It differs slightly in that Thomas was reputed to be a trader and that he had shot the dog. The rest of the story is identical.

[103] *Kaik* = southern Maori dialect for *kainga* or village.

One afternoon the Wakataupuka asked a lot of us if we'd like to go with him to the kaik to see the head, and as time hung heavily on our hands we all consented to go; but little did we know what he was up to. When we arrived at the kaik the Wakataupuka had some difficulty in getting the woman to show us the head, but he represented to her that the white people were very anxious to see it, so she brought it out. It seems that her husband was drowned at Oamaru, and the men who were with him at the time burnt his body but preserved his head to bring home to his widow.

When the woman brought out the head, she stuck a stick in the ground, put another stick across the top of that, put the head on that, then tied a mat around the neck. At a little distance it looked for all the world like a man sitting on the ground with a mat round him. The face too, unless on very close inspection, looked quite natural, and the hair was combed and oiled in true Maori fashion. The woman kept the head in such a pretty little house not far from her own door. It was painted fantastically with red ochre. The whole thing had something ghastly about it – bright sunshine on the beach, in the centre the corpse's head with staring, unseeing eyes, and around a motley group – astonished white men, some superstitious ones half-afraid, gaping children, sobbing and moaning women, admiring youths and maidens, and stolid, indifferent men.

One burly Maori, a relation of the dead man, was standing close by with a mere[104] in his hand. The Wakataupuka asked if he might look at it, and the Maori handed it to him at once, where upon he walked straight up to the head, caught it by the hair and was off with it down the beach before anyone guessed his intention. Oh it was terrible to hear those women, the way they mourned the loss of the head, groaning and moaning the most gruesome wails of distress and despair. We could hear them for ever so long. It was dreadful! I believe they kept it up till the *John Barry* sailed. Of course they could not raise an objection in any practical way to anything done by one so high in rank as the Wakataupuka.

---

[104] *Mere* = fighting club – often made from pounamu/greenstone.

Chief Wakataupuka, 1827. After John Boultbee.

# Chapter 18

*MAORI CUSTOMS – EMBALMING THE DEAD –*

*A NOTED CHIEF – SOME OF HIS DOINGS*

"Grandfather, please tell us more about the Wakataupuka," said Jack.

"Did they embalm all the Maoris in the olden days?" asked Fred.

"No Fred, only the most important ones were embalmed, and mothers often had their babies embalmed too. I remember seeing a baby that one mother had kept; it looked for all the world like a child asleep. She kept it in a pretty little house and only looked at it on fine days, as the damp spoilt it. They loved to look at the child's body and pray over it. I should think the Maoris were descended from the Egyptians; a good many of their fashions were the same[105]. But Jack wants to know more about the Wakataupuka, so I must tell you about him.

The Wakataupuka was a tyrant among his own people, but very good to a white man. I have often thought that under more favourable circumstances the Wakataupuka would have been a hero. Something of the Napoleon type, it is true; but he had many noble traits of character, though to his own people he was often cold-blooded and cruel.

Tiger Jack told me that once two boatloads of white people and a good number of Maoris – the Wakataupuka amongst them – went pigeon shooting up the Taieri. Towards evening they all came down to the boats again, laden with their day's spoil. One Maori was saying he wondered if a shot would kill a man as it would a pigeon, and the Wakataupuka overheard him. He ordered a Maori to go over to a tree a few yards off and the man, without a moment's hesitation, did

---

[105] William Thomas is referring to the idea of a shared Maori/Egyptian linguistic and artistic heritage. This theory was popularised in the late 19th century by researchers such as Edward Tregear (see the "*Aryan Maori*" 1885).

as he was bid, never thinking for a moment what his chief was going to do. The Wakataupuka then borrowed a gun from a white man, and before anyone guessed his intention, shot his man dead. Then handing back the gun he coolly remarked,

'Oh, shot will kill a man.'[106] Jack Tiger said he never could bear the sight of a pigeon after that.

In '34 Mr Weller had a whaleboat built, but it was a cranky affair and no good for whaling, so he sold it to Bloody Jack. Young Taiaroa – Maiapura they called him – was saying what a great man Jack was. He had two boats, while the Wakataupuka had only one.

'I've got two,' said Taupuka.

'No you've only got one,' persisted young Taiaroa.

So Wakataupuka said it was his boat lying at the kaik about a mile off; but Maiapura declared it belonged to Tuturakapawa.

'I lent it to Tuturakapawa to come down from Cloudy Bay, otherwise he'd have had to walk; but it's my boat,' said Wakataupuka, and he ordered his men to bring the boat up.

When the boat came there was no more said about it that night, and we all went off home to bed. The Wakataupuka had a little hut just next door to mine and at daylight next morning I knew there was going to be a great row. I heard the Wakataupuka's aide-de-camp come and tell him that the boat was gone – taken back to the kaik. He ordered the fellow to tell the men to bring it back. Just as I went outside the door, I met the Wakataupuka coming out of his door.

'Good morning,' I said, 'what's the matter?'

'Good morning,' he answered, 'nothing the matter – nothing, nothing at all.'

'There comes the boat.' I said.

---

[106] A variation of this story appeared in the Otago Witness (17 May 1905)

'Yes boat come, all right.' He was as unconcerned and cool as possible, and when we got to the beach just opposite Mr Weller's house, he waited quietly till the boat came up. Then he ordered the men to haul it up, and they fetched it up almost out of the water.

Presently from all quarters you could see the Maoris coming, armed to a man with meres and hatchets, and here and there a stray musket – they all had something.

Bloody Jack and his men were standing there. Jack didn't say a word either way, but they were all armed. Out of the mob rushed young Taiaroa, with a small carpenter's hammer in his hand and struck the boat twice on the bow. 'You hit that boat again just once,' roared the Wakataupuka, 'and I'll come down and drown you.'

He would have done it too, and young Taiaroa was wise enough to know that. Then a Maori carpenter named Kauti said something; I don't know what it was – I couldn't understand them very well in those days – but the Wakataupuka picked up a stave off a cask and hit the fellow across the shoulders, knocking him down, and called for his sword.

But the man with the sword was some way off and in all my life I never saw anybody pick themselves up as smartly as Kauti did that day, and he ran; and then they all ran, old and young – did they scamper. The Wakataupuka stood there flourishing his sword and it was funny to see them all flying from one man. It was high water too, and they all went splashing in almost up to their knees to get along the beach. Laugh! We laughed till we almost cried, and Mr Weller was calling out, 'Go Taupuka – go for it!'

Next year, '35, Wakataupuka died of the measles. He took ill when he was with us but insisted on going home to Rhuapuka. He started one afternoon and got as far as Bloody Jack's Island. He went ashore there and died. He ordered them to burn his body and bury his ashes – that was so that none of his enemies could come and take his bones to make fish-hooks of – a peculiar way they had of giving an insult and revenging themselves on the living by showing such disrespect for the dead."

# Chapter 19

*A GRIM TIT FOR TAT – HARRY MACKIE AND THE MAORIS*

*– FRANK THE CARPENTER*

"Grandfather, isn't there anything more you could tell us about the Wakataupuka?" demanded Jack.

"Nothing I can think of just now my boy," answered Grandfather. "Oh yes, though – I remember a trick he played on a fellow named Harry Mackie once, though he was generally so good to white people.

Harry Mackie had been the mate on a vessel with Captain Anglem once; but for some reason he stopped at Codfish to seal, and there he took a Maori wife. He never would call a Maori by his name, but it was always 'You cannibal here,' and 'You cannibal there,' with Mackie.

The Wakataupuka noticed this and asked what it meant. Some of the white people who could talk Maori explained to him what a cannibal meant.

'Oh that it?' said he, 'all right,' and he laughed. Such a low musical laugh he had too.

Harry Mackie was very fond of Maori cabbage[107] and muttonbird fat boiled, and whenever he came to Rhuapuka, the first thing he did was to get the women he knew to make this, his favourite dish. The Wakataupuka knew this so he said to the women:

'Next time Harry Mackie comes here and wants cabbage, you get the fat out of this kelp bag.' The bag indicated contained man's fat and it had been procured from an old Maori who was rather given to eating his fellow-men.

---

[107] Puha (sow thistle).

The women did not dare to disobey, and the next time he came, all of his boat's crew were just finishing their cabbage and muttonbird fat (as they thought) when up came the Wakataupuka.

'You the cannibal now, Harry Mackie,' said he.

'No,' said Mackie, 'I'm no cannibal but YOU are,' with a sneer.

Again the Wakataupuka laughed his low, amused laugh and kept saying, 'Harry Mackie cannibal; all right, Harry Mackie!'

Some of the others were a bit alarmed at this and inquired of the women what he meant. When they found out they were nearly all terribly sick and everyone said they were sure it shortened Harry Mackie's days.

Not long afterwards Jim Brown and Bloody Jack were helping him to move from Codfish to the Old Neck. One afternoon they landed on a small island over at Stewart Island and camped there. When they went to bed Mackie complained of great pains, and in two hours he was dead.

They put up at the head of his grave part of an old canoe, and a fellow that was with them, whom we always called 'Frank the Carpenter,' – I never knew him by any other name – carved his name, age, and the date of his death most beautifully. I have often seen the Yankees go ashore to look at it, for really it was a work of art.

When they lowered the coffin into the grave, Jack threw off his mat and let it fall in too – that would prevent any Maori from digging up the grave and eating the body when they saw his mat.

"But they didn't dig bodies up to eat them surely!" gasped Fred.

"Of course they did. I remember one notorious old cannibal named Karapipi dug up the body of Captain Strange and ate it after it had been buried for three weeks."

"The dirty old brute," said Jack, "Fred looks ready to cry, so tell us what became of Frank the Carpenter please."

"Well there's nothing very pleasant to tell about poor Frank either," said Grandfather, "In '35 I think it was, he went carpenting to Preservation for a chap named Jim Wareham. He and Wareham were always quarrelling about something, and did not get on very well together.

One morning the boats were going out and it was dreadfully rough. Just as they were starting, Wareham passed the remark to the others that he'd give Frank a good 'drilling' today, meaning plenty of disagreeable work and abuse. When they got as far as Anglem's Point the other boats stopped, but Wareham ran over to Codfish. Somehow or other his boat capsized. They all managed to scramble ashore, but Frank, poor fellow, who was drowned.

What Wareham had said seemed to prey on his mind terribly; he never dreamt that he'd repent his words so soon. He went to America shortly afterwards and was himself drowned in a storm off Newfoundland."

# Chapter 20

*AT WAIKAWA – INVITED TO RUB NOSES – MAORI GIRLS AND WOMEN*

"I'll tell you about an old Maori called Kaupatiti tonight, if you like boys," said Grandfather, so we all left what we were doing and came to his side.

"I had been down to Port Molyneux with Bloody Jack," he began, "and on our way home we called in at Waikawa; there was a fishery there[108], and in the afternoon we were in the headman's house, and I could see that one of our boat's crew, a Maori, was quite faint with hunger.

I said to the owner of the house, a Yankee named Mantell, 'You might let me give that poor boy something to eat.'

'Certainly,' he said, 'give him as much as he wants.

So I cut him off some pork and damper, and gave him a quart pot of tea, and he was sitting down quietly eating this when in came Jack. He asked the boy who gave him the food, and the lad told him that I did, so Jack turned to me and said: 'There will be a row when we get back to Rhuapuka.' So I asked him why.

'Because that boy has a tapu[109] on him. He's not allowed to eat in a house like this,' said Jack, 'wait till you see old Kaupatiti, his grandfather, and then you won't ask why.'

Kaupatiti was a high priest, or something among them. He was forever tapu-ing somebody, and woe betide the person who removed or discarded the tapu. I wouldn't have done it if I had known at the time, but I couldn't see the poor fellow half-starving, and I wasn't very frightened of his grandfather, though he was such a great man. He had more slaves, I believe, than any other person in the South Island.

---

[108] Just inside the Waikawa harbour entrance on the eastern shore.

[109] *Tapu* = a spiritual restriction.

When we were not quite three miles off the land, on old fellow in the boat started hollering to Kaupatiti what I'd done. We could see him trudging along the beach, with his stick in his hand, to where he knew we'd land. Of course it was a long time before he could understand, but while we were a good way off, the old fellow made out the meaning of what they nearly all by the this time were yelling to him. There was a strong wind blowing us ashore.

When we reached the beach he was about 100 yards off – we had reached the landing first – though we had been coming along the beach with him as it were.

Jack told me to take my bag and run for his house, for even Kaupatiti daren't go in there. So I shouldered my bag and ran for it, and he after me storming and fuming and brandishing his stick. I reached the house before he caught me, I stood just inside and he outside, as near as he dared to come, making such faces, poking out his tongue, cutting such cappers and fairly foaming at the mouth with rage.

He called out to Jack to know what this Pakeha's name was, and when Jack told him, his passion was over in a moment, and he wanted me to go out and 'nose' him.

But I wasn't going to 'nose' him for anything. You see, I was a regular white-headed boy among the Maoris, and they thought far more of me than I deserved[110].

You should have seen the Maoris when the boats came in, to see the Maori girls come to the beach to meet them. When we were whaling in Otago, there was one particular point they always came to, and they danced on the sand as we came in, singing and clapping their hands, and keeping time, 40 or 50 of them in a row, with their clean mats and shining hair adorned with chaplets of leaves and flowers. I suppose their ages ranged from 15 to 20. There were some beautifully graceful creatures among them too, but as a rule their eyes and teeth were their main features.

---

[110] William's status was possibly due to his marriage to the Tukuwaha, his friendship with Tuhawaiki and other connections and interactions with Maori (such as saving the life of the wounded Maori in Port Cooper, see Chapter 3).

But their dancing was really worth seeing, they kept such perfect time, and there was a certain graceful rhythm in their movements that I have never seen in European dancing.

The best of it was, they only came there to make fun of us. I used to feel very angry sometimes when we came in wet and hungry, to see all these creatures laughing at us; and the men would not hurry up and row as slowly as possible to they could watch these girls. There was one fellow in my boat – an Australia black – I don't know what his real name was, but he was always called Jimmy Mokomoko. The chorus of one of their songs was 'Jimmy Mokomoko, Jimmy Mokomoko – oh.' With a long drawn-out wail; and the fellow used to be awfully proud of this, though we found out as we got to know their ways, they were only bemoaning poor Jimmy's ugliness.

When I first came to N.Z. I was astonished to see how proud the Maori women were of their hair, and how well they kept it considering they had no combs. Yet they'd do up their hair and take out every tangle with one piece of stick, or a red-bill's beak. It must have taken them hours to do it though, but I suppose they had nothing else to do.

# Chapter 21

*AN EXCHANGE AT SEA – POTATOES FOR GROG – TRAGIC RESULTS*

"Tell us a yarn tonight Grandfather please." we all clamoured.

"Very well boys, I'll tell you about a voyage we made down to New Zealand in the latter end of February 1835.

We were just off the North Cape one day when we saw a schooner, and the captain asked me if I'd go aboard to see if they could spare us some potatoes. So we went on board and saw the schooner laden with timber heading to the Bay of Islands. I forget the schooner's name but she was a nice looking craft. I think the captain was as dandy a fellow as I ever saw. He had a big scar almost from his forehead to his neck, on one side of his face, which gave him a villainous look. It must have been a desperate gash; we heard afterwards that he received it on his way out from England. His crew mutinied and in the scuffle he was really well knocked about. When he reached Sydney he had his certificate taken from him, and was never allowed to take charge of a ship again.

Well this afternoon he said he couldn't sell us any potatoes, but that he'd give us a few, so he gave us two Maori baskets full, and I asked him if there was anything he would like in return. He said he'd like some grog, if we had any to spare, so I went back to the *Lucy Ann* and told Captain Anglem. He filled a five-gallon keg and took it aboard the schooner himself. That night the crew all got drunk and somehow or other they had a row with the captain, who struck some of them; then they, in their drunken frenzy threw him overboard. On reaching the Bay of Islands, the mate failed to report in time, and he was taken with the rest to Hobartown. The crew were all hanged and the mate was imprisoned for life.

But of course we knew nothing of this till long afterwards. The next day Captain Anglem asked me if I would go ashore with my boat's crew to try and get some potatoes from the natives.

I never gave it a thought that the Maoris might be savage, but one of my men refused to go, so the cooper volunteered to go instead.

We went into a little bay[111]. I think it was the most beautiful little place I ever saw. There was a splendid background, whilst in the foreground pumpkins and melons were growing almost to the water's edge. We all took a fancy to the place, and if we'd had a bad captain would never have gone back to the ship.

There were numbers of natives there but we couldn't understand a word they said. They appeared to understand us though, and seemed very friendly. They hauled our boat up and loaded it with pumpkin, melons, potatoes, and fruit of all kinds – more than we could carry.

After we had been there an hour or more we noticed the women making great preparations for a feast of some kind, so we thought it was time to go. We took a good deal of the stuff out of our boat and hauled it back into the water, when to our consternation, about 40 Maoris came and fairly carried the boat a good deal farther up than it had been before.

We all felt a bit scared, and the cooper – an Irishman – fairly trembled. For a few minutes I could not think what to do, then I remembered that Captain Anglem, who was fairly well acquainted with the Maori customs – had told me that if they ever meant foul play they sent the women and children away. There were plenty of women and children about so I felt safe, and told the others what Captain Anglem had told me.

Presently the Maoris beckoned us to come and have something to eat: so we went. We tried hard to eat what they gave us but, good gracious, they gave us each about enough for six men! However they didn't seem to object to our want of appetite, but packed up all that was left for us to take with us.

---

[111] Possibly the Maori village near Russell or Kororareka as it was known then. This was a popular provisioning port for early whalers in the Bay of Islands. Later on, as the settlement grew it gained a reputation as a lawless and bawdy port, earning the nickname 'Hellhole of the Pacific'. Deserting seamen, runaway convicts, grog sellers and prostitutes all made their homes there. The whalers bartered muskets for food and this probably encouraged the local Nga Puhi Chief Hongi Hika and the northern Maori to instigate local inter-tribal warfare.

At last we set off for the ship, accompanied by about 50 Maoris in canoes, and each had as much as it would hold of vegetables, fruit, flax and fresh pork, besides seven good sized pigs, which they insisted on us taking.

It was fun to see the faces of those on board as we came alongside. When the Maoris clambered up on deck they presented the things to Captain Anglem, who was very pleased, and wanted to make them some return. But all they took was one miserable little blanket, I don't believe you could buy such a small one now if you wanted to. It was simply ridiculous to see their delight – they danced about on deck till the poor *Lucy Ann* trembled again. They thought they had made a splendid bargain, poor things, and returned to their homes brimful of glee."

A whaling port in the Bay of Islands, mid 19<sup>th</sup> century. Unknown artist.

# Chapter 21 (continued)

*MUTINOUS CONVICTS – CAPTURE AND RECAPTURE -*

*A BOY'S PITIFUL FATE*

"I remember sometime in the '20's it was, a ship named the *Lady Wellington* was taking prisoners to Norfolk Island.

They had been out from Sydney two or three days, when the prisoners rose and took the brig. They put the soldiers and crew in chains below and took charge of the vessel themselves. One day they came into the Bay of Islands – for water I think. When the old pilot went on board the ship, he noticed the broad arrow on everything[112]. So when he had taken them in, he told Captain Duke, who was there in the whaler *The Sisters*, and Duke told him that when he took them out again he was to take them down between *The Sisters* and another whaler and that they would fire on the crew and take the *Wellington*. The pilot did that, and the brig was easily taken, for they had no ammunition, and only the arms that the soldiers had had – a few swords and cutlasses.

All the prisoners were chained and put below, and the soldiers and former crew restored. Captain Duke and the old pilot went with them to Sydney.

There were nine respites amongst them, and they were all hanged, the rest of the prisoners (about 15 in number) getting life sentences. One of the respites was a boy about 16 years old.

In those days the gaol in Sydney was overhung on one side by a street which was a little higher than the wall, though sufficiently far away to prevent communication in any underhand way. Yet from this street one could see quite plainly into the prison yard and hear what was said too.

---

[112] The 'broad arrow' stamped on all convict clothes and equipment indicated the items were 'crown property'.

When the morning of the execution came, a tremendous crowd gathered to see the ghastly sight. Most of them made some sort of speech before they were executed, and they all swore that the boy had nothing to do with the taking of the brig; also they intended no harm to those they put below, for they meant to land them the day after being in the Bay of Islands.

But it was no use saying anything. One after the other they were hanged till at last the boy's turn came. Never can I forget that scene. He stood motionless for a moment, till the captain put his hand kindly on the lad's shoulder, and then he turned and looked at the silent crowd above him. There was a slight breeze blowing and it lifted the bright golden curls from his high forehead. He looked round fearlessly enough, with a bright and brave look on his face.

With a wave of his hand he began, 'It is likely,' he said, 'that I should lie now, for in a few moments I shall meet the living God. I do not fear death; but still I swear that I am as innocent as a baby of what I was brought out from England for, and, as all of the others have said before me, I am innocent of any part in taking the brig. And I am to be hanged like a dog! Oh mother, mother!'

For an instant his composure forsook him and he wept like a child. The chaplain comforted the poor boy. And small wonder that he broke down – to be hanged just when for every boy life should be its brightest.

The crowd was much moved, and scarcely an eye was dry. Women sobbed, men groaned, and from the seething mass the cry rose again and again:

*'A reprieve! A reprieve! Ask the Governor for a reprieve!'*

Might as well ask a stone wall! Everyone knew it was useless, and the hangman was impatient to have finished his task. The boy quickly recovered himself, and looking around again said, 'May God forgive all those concerned in my death, for I do.'

The chaplain spoke a few words to him, the rope was placed around his neck, the board he was standing on removed, his hands clasped as if in prayer, and then – it was over!

I have never seen a crowd so deeply affected, and that old pilot had to be put under the protection of the police all the time he was in Sydney, or I believe they would have killed him.

I often saw him down in New Zealand afterwards, and if Tommy Chasland was drunk, he always gave him a rough turn about that poor boy.

Sydney gallows, 19th century. Unknown artist.

# Chapter 22

*AN OLD-TIME SNOWSTORM – BILL GAYLEY AND THE YANKEES –*

*SOME GRUESOME SIGHTS*

"Grandfather, it's snowing hard," cried Jack the other day in a delighted tone, "do come and see."

"So it is my boy," Grandfather answered. "It reminds me of the heavy fall we had in Otago in '36. It lasted for three days, snowing day and night. It was the heaviest fall of snow I have ever seen in New Zealand.

I remember it was at its worst on the 4th July. There were three Yankee whalers in Otago then – the *Columbus*, the *Martha*, and the *Mechanic* – besides a Sydney whaler and our two large shore parties[113]. All of us went up to Mr Weller's house to help the Yankees celebrate the Glorious Fourth, and we did have some fun too – snowballing, singing, dancing, and carousing to our heart's content.

My boatsteerer, Bill Gayley, sang a song that none of them ever heard before, called '*The American Star*'. It was ridiculous to see the Yankees delight. They jumped as if they were mad. Gayley had to sing it again and again, and they nearly all wrote out a copy of it. No mistake, Gayley had a magnificent voice – so powerful yet so wonderfully sweet. He used to sing the Grimaldi[114] songs delightfully. I believe he was offered large sums of money to become a professional singer, but he always refused.

---

[113] The *Columbus* and the *Martha* were based in Otago throughout 1836; the *Mechanic* spent much of the year at Port Underwood, Cloudy Bay but was recorded to travelling around the South Island around that time.

[114] Nicolo Grimaldi, a 17th-18th century opera singer/actor who was associated with renowned composer George Handel.

I don't know who Gayley originally was, for, unlike most of the men, he never mentioned his early life, but I am sure he was a gentleman by birth. He was awfully fond of telling about when he was captain of the forecastle on board the *Royal Sovereign* in the Battle of Algiers[115]. I'd often heard him wax eloquent about the attack they made one afternoon. They fired a broadside of shot on the natives ashore, and before the poor wretches recovered from their astonishment thousands of them were killed and presently the water running past was the colour of blood.

The Algerian guns were cemented in, otherwise they could have elevated or lowered them, they could have sunk the man-of-war. As it was they fired on the *Royal Sovereign* and knocked two of her ports into one, and she would have been sure to sink but that the Admiral[116] signalled another ship to go and take some of the fire off her. Next morning the Admiral sent his first lieutenant ashore with a flag of truce (and here Gayley generally melted into tears) he was received by the enemy with no great pleasure.

'Couldn't King George have sent me anything better than a beardless boy?' he was asked.

'Oh,' replied the lieutenant, 'if he thought you wanted something with a beard, no doubt he'd have sent you a billy goat.'

'No insolence,' growled the old Turk, 'or I'll put you into one of those guns and fire you off.'

'Do,' said the lieutenant, 'and see those ships out there? Well they'll make me a grand funeral pyre.'

---

[115] The *Royal Sovereign* was not recorded at the Bombardment of Algiers (1816), so perhaps William recalled the wrong ship from Gayley's past. The story's narrative suggests Gayley may have served on the flagship *HMS Queen Charlotte*, named for the then Royal Highness (which may explain the mix up). Other than that the tale is generally quite accurate. If Gayley was Captain of the Forecastle he would have been in command of two cannon and two carronades.

[116] Edward Pellew - Lord Exmouth.

However after the Christian slaves were freed, a good number were brought on board the *Royal Sovereign*. Gayley said he never in all his life saw such a pitiful sight.

Plenty of them had their tongues cut out, and they were all more or less disfigured with hard work and ill-usage. In the end Gayley was proud of his service on the *Royal Sovereign*. His singing was a real treat though. I've seen Mr Weller, when he was dying, drag himself out of bed to hear Bill sing."

"Grandfather," said Bertie, "I can't get over that poor boy you told us about that was hanged. How could you go and see him?"

"It was just habit child, I suppose. Hanging was so common in those days that one thought no more of looking on that you do now when you see a drunken man dragged off to the police station. I was only about seven when I first saw a hanging case. My father made me go to see it. All children went in those days; it was thought to be a warning to them not to do the same thing. For it is not the love of good but the fear of evil that keeps the criminal class down, so my father always said.

There were nine men handed that morning. There had been ten connected with crime – a brutal murder and robbery – but one man turned King's evidence[117] and escaped. They were taken out in a bullock cart to Cascade – a place about two miles out of Hobartown. They sang hymns all the way out. They were followed by crowds of people.

Before this, all the hanging had been done on a tree, but now for the first time a gallows was erected. Some of them were Romanists, and they had a priest there as well as Parson Bedford. It was dreadful to hear them praying and crying to their God for mercy. It was a terribly harrowing scene, and it sunk deep into my childish heart.

---

[117] "King's evidence" is the act of testifying against an accomplice to receive a more lenient sentence.

For weeks and months I could think of nothing else, and it was ever before my mind's eye. One after another they were all hanged. They all died characteristically – some feigning indifference and running laughingly up the steps, and others again thoroughly unnerved and hysterically screaming, struggling and crying.

And then the last man's turn came. He was a huge, burly, red-headed man, and as he swung out the rope broke and he fell to the ground. The hang man ran round and picked the fellow up quite unhurt. Then Major Bell, overseer of the executions took to his horse and galloped into town to ask the Governor for a reprieve. The Governor seemed inclined to grant it, but his wife (Mrs. Sorell) would not hear of it. While Mr Bell was away a dead silence reigned on the assembled crowd, till the clatter of horse's hoofs was heard again, and the suspense was over. The fellow made no sign, but accepted his fate with stolid indifference. The rope did not break the second time, but the drop fell and killed a dog that was standing near it. A moan went through the crowd. The bodies were put into a bullock cart and taken to Hobartown for burial there. I remember clinging to my father, sobbing and trembling with grief and horror. The man who turned King's evidence had a dreadful time of it. The boys, and even the men used to stone him, and he had to leave the place for fear of his life."

# Chapter 23

*AN OLD-TIME RAID – NORTH VS. SOUTH –*

*CHRONICLES OF RHUAPUKA – A SANGUINARY RECORD*

"Grandfather you'll tell us a yarn tonight won't you?" we all asked.

"Yes if you like boys. I'll tell you about the time when a band of Maoris walked over here from Nelson for the purpose of taking what they could out of the south.

Three of us – Jack Carter, Jim Brown and myself – were waiting at Rhuapuka for Captain Bruce to come to his brig, the *Merrimac*, to take away our oil. It was dreadful weather; but Bloody Jack and some little Maori boys came over from the Bluff in Spencer's boat. We could see that Jack was dreadfully upset about something, and presently he told us that 50 or 60 Maoris were at Tuturau, and that the chief, an old fellow they called the Pauhou[118], had killed and eaten a little child about three years old. Of course all the southern Maoris were up in arms, and Jack had come to Rhuapuka to gather together all his forces. It was quite amusing to see the old men and women digging and packing up potatoes; and next day all that were able set off with Jack to the mainland.

We wanted to go with them very badly, but Jack wouldn't hear of it. He said that if anything happened to us the white people would come down on him for it. So we didn't like to press him any further, though we were young then and were

---

[118] Te Puoho-o-te-rangi, Ngati Tama (northern Taranaki). Allied to Te Rauparaha and Ngati Toa. In the mid-1830s Te Puoho led a migration to Golden Bay in the Nelson region. There he formulated a plan to attack southern Maori, in his words to Te Rauparaha to "scale the fish" (the South Island) from top to bottom. He set off down the West coast with around 50 men. The party moved inland through the Haast Pass, down the Makarora Valley to Lake Wanaka, through the mountains of Central Otago and finally emerged on to the Waimea Plains of Southland. They halted to recoup at Tuturau, a small lamprey fishing hamlet just south of Mataura. It was there that Tuhawaiki's counter attack was sprung and Te Puoho was shot. See Atholl Anderson's "*Te Puoho's Last Raid*" (1996) for further details.

longing for the fun and excitement of a fight. We gave them our guns and rifles[119], for they were very short of firearms, and only had one double-barrelled gun amongst them.

One morning just at dawn the two tribes met – just about where the paper mill is now. The Pauhou discharged his gun, several other shots were discharged, and the northern chief was killed[120]. After that the others were easily taken prisoners. Jack said as the invaders had come with the intention of killing them, he though the best thing to do was to kill the invaders. But a good many of the others begged for the lives of their enemies. Old Taiaroa took the young chief Tekuri[121] to Otago and released him; and Jack agreed to make slaves of them all.

So he took them over to Rhuapuka and gave them ground to build on and where they could make gardens. There were a good many women among the prisoners, and it was their fashion on making an expedition of that sort that all the men of any note should take their wives with them to share their hardships. There was a girl with them too, about 15 years old; she had been brought to eat, but they had kept putting off the killing because she was so thin. But on the way down they said the old chief killed dozens of men to eat. If there were no strangers about, he'd order one of his own men to be killed. They got on comfortably at Rhuapuka for some time. They nearly all lived together, but some of them were scattered about with different families, and Captain Bruce had one old man making a garden for him over at Bluff.

---

[119] A six barrelled revolving flintlock rifle associated with Tuhawaiki can be seen at the Otago Museum. Thomas family tradition suggests this rifle may have been one of the weapons mentioned above.

[120] Te Puoho was reputedly killed by the young chief Topi Patuki (known as John Topi in the yarns). Following Tuhawaiki's death, Topi would become the paramount chief of Murihiku.

[121] William has confused 'Te Kuri' with chief Te Kiore Paremata Te Wahapiro who was taken to Otakou by Taiaroa. According to some accounts Taiaroa felt obliged to save Paremata due to Te Puoho allowing Taiaroa and his warriors to depart the siege of Kaiapoi several years earlier.

About Christmas time in 1836, a schooner over at Stewart Island came near Rhuapuka from Port William. The captain was always at this Maori settlement, and somehow he made it up with them to get them off in the night and get them back to Nelson.

So one morning, lo and behold, every Maori in the kaik was gone. And they'd taken all their food with them. They were well underway before daylight. The Rhuapuka Maoris gave chase in four or five big boats, but it was impossible to overtake the schooner, so they had to return. They were angry too. They killed Jack's man before he came home (Jack was in Sydney), and they would have killed all the others too, but their masters protected them.

When Jack came home he was angry that his man had been killed and said that the others must be treated the same; but Captain Bruce paid £5 to save his man's life, and Mrs Topi refused to let her slave be killed, and they didn't dare go against her, as she was Wakataupuka's sister, so in the end there were only two others killed. One old fellow sat down on the beach and asked his master to kill him. So the master took a tomahawk and struck him on the back of the neck two or three times.

The other fellow took to his heels and ran, and three others ran after him. For about half a mile he kept ahead of them, but in crossing some water he slipped and fell, and they overtook him. He carried a short tomahawk and the other men had meres. One fellow disabled the runaway's right arm otherwise he'd have killed them all I believe. As it was he gave one fellow some rare gashes, but three to one wounded man. He was soon killed, poor fellow.

Jack was angry because they didn't kill them English fashion, and shoot them; but the Maoris preferred their own fashion of butchering, so they had their own way."

# Chapter 24

*THE NEW RIVER IN 1837 – WHALING SHIPS AT THE BLUFF –*

*THE LATE DR MENZIES – A WHOLESALE LAND SALE –*

*TAKING A RISE OUT OF MR MANTELL*

"Grandfather, is there anything more you can tell us about the Pauhou?" asked Jack.

"Well boy, considering he was dead, I don't suppose there is; but I know he gave all the Southern Maoris a dreadful scare. I remember when we first came to the New River – in '37 it was. It was hard work to get any Maoris to come with us at all, they were so afraid of another invasion. All the Maoris had left the mainland and gone either to Rhuapuka or Centre Island[122] to live. Carter and I had our fishery where the pilot station now is[123], and Jack Williams and Joss had another higher up the river[124]. We came over in February and went to Otatara to get totara bark to build our huts with.

The country was then as wild as you could wish to see it – all bush and swamp. If anyone had suggested that any of us should live to see Invercargill such a town as it is, we should have smiled. As it was, we never imagined that people would ever settle here.

I was reading a letter in Monday's Times about the early settlers which said in the '30s and early '40s as many as 12 whaling ships had been lying in Bluff Harbour at a time, and I know for a certainty that there was never more than four at the most. The letter also mentioned Tom Brown's 'exciting scenes in following

---

[122] Known to Maori as Rarotoka, the southern Maori dialect for Rarotonga.

[123] Near the present day settlement of Omaui.

[124] At Oue, Sandy point.

up and harpooning whales.'[125] I could not help laughing at that, for I remember in '36 – two years after I came to New Zealand – Tom Brown went with Captain Bruce in the *Sydney Packet* to Sydney to be christened, when he was a baby, so he can hardly be called an old hand. Why, there's Captain Gilroy at the Bluff who was here as boat steerer before Tom Brown knew what a whale was! I think Gilroy came in '37 with Captain Bradley in the *Protest*.

I remember too when Dr Menzies[126] came here, but it wasn't till '53. One afternoon he and Mr Mantell, the commissioner, a constable, and four Maoris arrived having walked from Otago. They were all pretty well knocked up, but Dr Menzies was the worst – his clothes were torn to shreds and his boots were almost gone.

Mr Mantell and the constable stayed at Mr Spencer's, but the doctor came down to Jack Tiger's[127] hut, where we all were. It was very rough, but he seemed thankful for any kind of shelter, and he asked if he could buy a pair of trousers anywhere. We couldn't help laughing at the idea, but I said to Jack – 'You've got a pair; give them to him.'

'Yes I've got an extra pair,' said Jack, 'but they're moleskins, and he's a doctor.'

'Oh,' I said, 'doctor or no doctor, he'd like a whole pair of trousers,' so Jack gave them to him, and he seemed very gratefully to get them. We bathed his feet in warm water and the siftings of the wheat we had just ground. He seemed much relieved, and the next morning he seemed considerably better.

But the Maoris who came down with them used to make fun of Dr Menzies, and take him off to the life. He hadn't the knack of bush travelling and used to go

[125] The letter in the Southland Times can also be read in Otago Witness, 4 October 1894, p. 14.

[126] Dr. James Alexander Robertson Menzies (b.1821 – d.1888). Dr Menzies travelled from Scotland to New Zealand in 1853 and journeyed with Mantell who was travelling to Bluff to make the final payments on the Murihiku purchase. Menzies eventually took up a 38,000 acre run on the lower Mataura River and was the first Superintendent of Southland when it split from Otago in 1861.

[127] Jack "Tiger" Macgregor.

at it that hard that he tore his boots to shreds.  A Maori offered to make him a pair of pararas[128] to wear, to save both his boots and feet, but he wouldn't have them, and I think after that they felt no pity for him, but delighted in laughing at him.

Next day there was the great land sale, when Mr Mantell bought all this end of New Zealand for the N.Z. Government for £1000. Mr Mantell sat just inside Spencer's house. He had a little table and chair there, and the Maoris went in, in their turn to receive their share. One man from Rhuapuka went in and Mr Mantell handed him ten pounds.

'My share 40 pounds,' said the man.

'No,' said Mr Mantell, 'you're only down for ten pounds. If you were down for forty I'd give you forty.'

So the man said. 'You can keep your ten – I don't want it. John Topi promised that I'd have forty.'

He went outside in an awful rage, and Mantell came to the door and said, 'Well I hope there's no grog about. I don't want any of the Maoris to get drunk.'

'No,' said Gilroy, 'I don't think you will find a glass of grog in the Bluff and I know there's none in that ship there either.'

Mr Mantell said he was very glad and went inside again; it was a good thing too. If there had been grog about someone would have been killed that day, for there was great quarrelling among the natives.

That afternoon we were all in Spencer's boatshed, when we saw Mr Mantell coming up the path. Some of the boys saw him coming and they knotted some tussocks across the path. Mr Mantell was short-sighted or something – anyway he wore spectacles, and he was looking up at us in the shed, and not noticing where he was walking.

---

[128] *Parara* = Maori flax sandals.

Presently there was a crash and a wild flourish of arms and legs in the air, and the spectacles flying in all directions. He was naturally such a dignified man that it was really more than human nature could stand without a good laugh, and we fairly roared; and the little Maori children who had caused the downfall tumbled about like the small niggers in Uncle Tom's Cabin[129] in piles of immeasurable giggles. It was a funny sight though. And when he picked himself up again and was terribly angry, this only added to their amusement, for the little beggars had a keen sense of the ridiculous."

Dr Menzies, 1889. Photographer Ross.    Walter Mantell, 1870. Photographer Clarke

---

[129] *Uncle Tom's Cabin; or, Life Among the Lowly* (1852) is an anti-slavery novel by American author Harriet Beecher Stowe.

# Chapter 25

*A LONELY COUPLE – MAORI V. EUROPEAN BURIALS –*

*WAIAU EPISODES – ADVENTURE IN MOKIS*

"Grandfather, what is the yarn going to be about tonight?" questioned Dick.

"I didn't know that I was to tell you one," answered Grandfather, "but I suppose if I don't I'll get no peace all the evening.

I was thinking tonight of an old Maori who lived with his wife for years at the mouth of the Big River[130]. It must have been dreadfully lonely, all by themselves, but they never seemed to feel it. There they lived in a little mimi[131], and caught fish and birds and eels.

Occasionally they received visits from other natives, for there was a Maori settlement at the Waiau in those days, but the visits were few and far between. At last, Old Mike, as he was called, got very old, the natives came from Centre Island and made him go with them to end his days. He was very loath to go, but in the end they persuaded him.

One afternoon Gregory and I were going to a look-out point to look for whales, and we saw Old Mike digging his wife's grave in the sand. She had died the previous night, and there the poor old man had her lashed up in her mat, ready for burial, and was patiently scraping away with a paua shell to get the grave deep enough. I offered to help him, but he refused, preferring to do everything for her himself. In those days the Maori used to bury their dead in a sitting posture, though they gave it up when they saw the white people's method.

---

[130] Near the head of Lake Hakapoua in Fiordland about 30 km east of Preservation Inlet.

[131] *Maimai* is an aboriginal word meaning small hut. The name now refers to duck-shooter's shelters.

That was the first and last time I ever saw a person buried like that. Gregory and I could do nothing else, so we stood by with bared heads till Old Mike had finished his sorrowful task. He seemed much gratified by our attentions, and came away quietly with us when it was all over.

There were a good many Maoris living about the Waiau then, five or six miles from the mouth. One afternoon three Maori women were trying to cross in a moki; but the current was very strong, and they were carried on and on, past one landing place and then another, trying in vain to steer to the opposite bank. At last they were carried out to sea, but they just drifted about, not very far from shore, tossing about the surf. There was no wind to carry them out, and for three days and three nights about within sight of their homes and their people, for all the Maoris watched on shore day and night. But they could do nothing. They had not even a canoe, and it is never very smooth on that beach either, and it took little enough to smash a canoe at any time.

At last a wind set in from the westward, and the moki was driven ashore, but only one woman was on her. The others, overcome by hunger and exposure had either dropped off or been washed away. The woman who survived was very weak and ill for a long time."

"Grandfather, whatever is a moki?" asked Jack.

"A moki is a raft made of bundles of koradi[132], my boy, made while the koradi is dry. The Natives used to use them on all the rivers to bring down their birds and eels and flax. I have seen them, when they were first made, carry a ton.

It was grand fun coming down the Waiau on one. How it used to spin! The only danger was in bumping against the bank or in running on to a snag. The current is so strong and swift that I was always glad to have someone else steer. But it was splendid fun, and the spice of danger made it all better. Of course a moki can only drift or be propelled in shallow water by pole – there was no way of rowing.

---

[132] *Koradi / korari* = flax stalks.

Once we were whaling at the Mataura when one day we saw a whale ashore on the other side of the river. The boats were away, and I didn't know how to get across. Some of the Maoris said they knew where there was a moki, a little way up the river, so I asked them to go for it. Off they went and presently returned with the moki. It was a very old one and quite watersodden; but we got across in it all right – 13 of us altogether, counting a boy.

We cut the bone out of the whale's head and dragged it up above high water mark. After we had finished we attempted to re-cross the river, but this was not so easily done.

In a little while the water came up over the moki and kept rising higher and higher. If they had only sat still I believe we would have got across all right. But no – they wouldn't. They all jumped to their feet, and that sent the moki further under.

She was sinking fast, and only three of us could swim, so I said to the other two who could swim – 'Let's swim ashore and get flax to tow the others in,' and turning to the others I said – 'Now, you keep perfectly still. It's your only chance.'

And they obeyed like Britons too – not one lost his head, not even the boy – not a move out of any of them. We got the flax as quickly as possible and returned to the sinking moki. We had some little difficulty in fastening it on underwater, but we managed it, and then swam ashore, and towed them all safely in with the knotted flax. I did feel relieved when I saw all safely ashore."

# Chapter 26

*IN CHALKY INLET – RESCUING THE PERISHING –*

*A SAILOR'S NARROW ESCAPE – BOB BLACKWELL'S FATE –*

*JACK SOLID'S FRIGHT.*

"Grandfather you promised to tell us a yarn tonight, you remember?" said Fred

"Yes my lad, so I did, but I will have to think first. I'm afraid I've told you all the yarns I know. Let me see – did I tell you about the chaps we picked up in Chalky one night?"

"No."

"Well I'll tell you about that.

It was in '48. We were three or four days in Chalky, weather bound. In fact we couldn't have got out if we tried, for the wind was blowing dead in from the S.W.

One afternoon we were all lounging about doing nothing when we saw a schooner coming in, and she was scudding[133] too. I said to my boat crew that if they liked we'd go down and meet the schooner, and see who she was, for we knew she wouldn't be coming into the arm we were in, for it was too narrow. So off we started. They were all Maoris in my crew except a man called Tom Leech. It was blowing tremendously, and the vessel passed us before we could get out to her; so we hoisted our sail and followed in her track. We hadn't gone far when I saw some dark object in the water just ahead of us.

'Why bless me Tom,' said I, 'but there's a man in the water!'

---

[133] Swiftly skimming along on the water.

'Man be blowed,' said Tom politely, 'you're dreaming. Where's a man to come from?'

'Wait a minute my boy,' said I, and with a few more strokes we were beside the unfortunate man, who was making a last faint struggle for life. 'Haul him in Tom,' I said, 'He's only a dream you know, so he won't weigh much.'

Tom growled something as he and two of the Maoris hauled the man in. He was a fine, powerfully built young man with a pleasant face; but just then he was unconscious, and all but dead. After a time he came round though, and looked at us in bewilderment. I explained to him how he came to be on our boat.

'God reward you all.' He said, his teeth chattering, and he was shivering from head to foot. Then he told us that he had been in the boat in tow behind the ship, to steer her, but not having much idea how to manage, as the boat had pitched and tossed, he was jerked out.

His shipmates did not find out that he was missing until they had anchored and were hauling up the boat. When we came alongside the schooner, it was just dark. The crew were all standing about in knots discussing the melancholy fate of their mate. They didn't seem to hear us, so I told the fellow to go aboard and change his wet clothes.

He swung himself up on deck and walked silently forward among his companions. They all fell back in astonishment too great for words. They thought it was a ghost, and he didn't look unlike one either, with his pale face and damp hair clinging to his forehead. The men stood gazing at him with eyes and mouths wide open and one fellow nearly fainted.

We couldn't help laughing as we watched them. Even the Captain looked terrified, but he went up to the man, and he told him how he managed to survive. He showed him the boat alongside which had picked him up, he came over, and I then recognised Captain Bailey, an old friend, and his schooner the *Fortitude*.

We all went aboard to supper then. The captain was very thankful that we had picked up his man, as he was feeling very miserable about his supposed death. And yet he knew that it would be useless to go back and look for him.

It was a dangerous job to get though, unless you thoroughly understand the job and are a good steerer. I remember when I was a very small boy hearing about a man who lost his life in that way. The man's name was Bob Blackwell, and he was coming out of Wedge Bay[134] behind a Government brig, when he was pitched out of the boat and never seen again. I always remembered that, and once, a long time afterwards, it came back to me very clearly.

It was one night we were coming out of Bull Bay[135], they put me in the boat behind the ship to steer. But I didn't want to steer, so I hauled in the steer oar and played out 50 or 60 fathoms of line, so that I could be towed at a safe distance. Then, though I was wet to the skin, I curled myself up in the bow of the boat and went fast asleep, and I slept until we reached Hobartown too. When they anchored and I failed to put in an appearance, they felt sure I was drowned. But when they hauled up the boat and a big heavy Yorkshire man stepped on me, I sprang up, almost knocking him overboard.

The poor fellow did get a fright, believing me dead, as he did. I don't know what his proper name was. We always called him Jack Solid – he was so heavy physically and mentally. I don't believe he was ever known to smile. That night he and I had to stay aboard the schooner until daylight, wet and hungry, and without a blanket or any food. Whaling wasn't child's play, I can tell you that boys."

"What made you go whaling?" inquired Jack.

"Well, I suppose I was not at all a good learner and had nowhere else from school to go." answered Grandfather.

---

[134] Wedge Bay is 10km west of Port Arthur, Tasmania.

[135] Bull Bay on Bruny Island was a major Tasmanian whaling station from around 1829 until 1843. It is also home to Derwent lighthouse, Tasmania's oldest lighthouse built in the 1830s.

# Chapter 27

*GRANDFATHER'S BOYHOOD – EARLY DAYS IN SYDNEY –*

*STORIES OF GOVERNOR KING – HOW THE CONVICTS FOUND CHINA –*

*A CRUEL JEW – BUTTERFLIES GALORE*

"Grandfather, you promised to tell us about when you were a little boy," said Bertie.

"So I will Bertie, but I'm sorry to say I wasn't a good boy, like you are, but a very mischievous, naughty one – something like Jack. I was born in Sydney on 17th March, 1811. Our house was in George Street, just opposite the old barrack gate.

My father was a Devonshire man, or rather boy, for he left England when very young. His uncle persuaded him to go on a voyage to America, holding out every inducement that would appeal to a boy's mind. But the reality proved very different from what he had been led to expect, and my father was made to do anything his uncle chose. Well, they made their way to America, and coming back they called in at some small port with timber. As my father was sitting disconsolately on the wharf, a recruiting sergeant came up and asked him if he'd enlist. He agreed gladly and walked off with the sergeant. He joined the 17th Light Dragoons, and being a splendid horseman he fell easily into the ways of the regiment. I've often heard my father say that though the daily round was irksome and not very easy, it was paradise to what his life had been on his uncle's ship.

Well after a time he was sent out to Sydney as orderly to Governor Bligh[136], who however did not keep his billet long.  Then Governor King[137] came –

---

[136] Governor Bligh (b.1754 – d.1817) is perhaps more famously remembered as the strict captain of the mutinous *Bounty* in 1789. His subsequent career as a Governor (1805-1808) led to Bligh being deposed during the Rum Rebellion. William Thomas senior was actually transported to Sydney for highway robbery and assault, see page 10.

[137] Captain Philip Gidley King (b.1758 – d.1808), Governor of New South Wales from 1800-1806. King appointed Major Joseph Foveaux (after whom Foveaux Strait was named for) as Lieutenant-Governor of Norfolk Island.

everybody liked him. He had been a sailor, when not suffering from gout, and was very genial and humorous. One peculiarity he had though. You see in those days any free person could have several convicts for servant free of charge, and even if they held a very good character could have the prisoner, and his rations out of the Government store besides. Well if anyone came and asked the Governor for a 'Government man,' he would refuse to give them one; but if they asked for an 'assigned servant,' he'd give them one in a minute.

Nobody quite understood the meaning of this, but I suppose he didn't like being continually reminded that he was only the Governor of a penal settlement. One morning a woman who owned a little property, came to him with the usual request for a Government man.

'What's your name?' asked Governor King.

'Agnes Thawley, sir.' She said

'Yes, but haven't you another name – what do they call you in town?'

The poor creature stammered and stuttered for a time. (She had a peculiar walk, or rather trot, and the boys nicknamed her The Pony). At last she said:

'Well, they call me The Pony.'

'Well,' said the Governor, laughing, 'trot you hussy, trot!' and off she had to go, too.

Another day a man came and asked for a 'Government man'. He was a fine handsome man, and the Governor said to him, 'What trade have you followed all your life, my man?'

The man drew himself up a trifle proudly, and answered that he was a soldier.

'A soldier!' repeated the Governor, 'Oh well, let me put you through a few marching exercises.' So he kept the fellow drilling away there for about a quarter of an hour. At last he got the man with his face towards the gate.

'Quick march!' shouted the Governor, and the man was down the path and on to the road before he realised that he had been made a fool of.

There were a number of Irishmen who were very bad in Sydney at the time. There were a great many prisoners, and they were mutinous and also ignorant. I've heard, though I won't say that it's quite true, that once about 100 of them decided to run away. The rations were served out once a week, and they all started with a week's provisions to WALK TO CHINA. They walked and walked, and got no great distance off from Sydney. Of course there was nobody living out in the country then; but one morning one jolly Irishman woke up and heard a cock crow. He roused the others and they gave three cheers, for they were sure they weren't far off China then. So they all got up and started walking again, but that morning they walked into the arms of the soldiers and police who had been out looking for them, and they were marched back into Sydney.

One night my father was riding along and he heard cries of 'Murder, murder!' coming from the direction of some bushes at the side of the road. He rode over to see what it was, but he had no business to do so, for he was carrying despatches, and he found a Jew named Ikey Bull beating a prisoner terribly with the butt of a gun.

Of course he took them both into Sydney with him. The prisoner was so badly hurt that father had to put him on his horse and walk himself. It happened about two miles from Sydney, so of course he was a good deal behind the expected time.

Governor King came running out to meet him 'Oh I'm glad to see you're safe,' he said, 'but what's all this?'

My father explained.

'Well,' said the Governor, 'as it happens it was a good thing you prevented a murder, but it wasn't your duty, you know. It might only have been a trap laid for you; each time you go I'm frightened you won't come back alive.'

Things were rather unsettled for some time, and provisions were getting low in the country, so the Governor said he thought everyone should go on an allowance. He was willing to go on the same allowance himself, and let everything be equal.

But Colonel Johnson, of the 23rd wouldn't hear of it. He wanted the prisoners and others to go on a half allowance, and the soldiers to still keep full allowance. You know, then in Sydney there was a large Government store, and everything that came into the country went there – it didn't matter to whom it belonged. Whatever goods a man brought, they had to go into the store, and he could only take out a weekly allowance. He had no more power to take out more than his allowance than a man who hadn't the faintest claim to the goods. Well the Governor and the colonel quarrelled away about the provisions till the colonel put the Governor under arrest and took charge himself[138].

Of course news couldn't be cabled home every day then but when information was received in England, a ship was sent out to bring both the Governor and Colonel home to have the case tried.

The case went against Colonel Johnson of course. His sword was broke over his head, he was disgraced and ordered to never draw sword again in Her Majesty's service. Colonel Johnson came out to Sydney again, where he had left his wife and family. He was a very rich man and had a lot of property in Sydney. He had a beautiful place some distance out of Sydney. My sister and I went there to stay once – before, of course, there was any disagreement. We had a splendid time. One thing I always remember distinctly was that Blanche Johnson, the eldest girl, had a room full of insects – dead ones of course. There were gorgeous butterflies pinned all over the walls, and I never tired of gazing at them.

---

[138] This incident became known as the Rum Rebellion of 1808 and was more about political power than illicit trade in alcohol or provisions as William recounts. It was only successful armed takeover of Australian government. Major (later Colonel) George Johnson and Major John MacArthur overthrew Governor Bligh. Bligh was temporarily replaced by Foveaux, after whom Foveaux Strait is named.

When Colonel Johnson came out again, he wrote to the English Government offering to find 1000 men and mount them of 1000 white horse to guard the country – in fact, to keep a small standing army at his own expense. But his offer was declined. They would have nothing whatever to do with him. A great many people were sorry to lose Governor King. He was well liked indeed. Before this his son had gone to England and applied to the Government there for a cutter to go through Torres Straits with, and to cruise around Australia. It was granted to him, and he came out in his smart little cutter, the *Mermaid*. He went through Torres Strait and right round Australia. He was the first to make the trip, and was knighted for it. He was a fine young fellow too, and very popular.

I haven't told you much about my doings after all, but I will go on tomorrow night."

Lt. Colonel George Johnson, 1810. Unknown artist.

# Chapter 28

*GOVERNOR MCQUARRIE – A TRAGIC EPISODE –*

*MIKE HOWE THE BUSHRANGER –*

*A GHASTLY SIGHT – SCHOOLBOY TROUBLES*

"Grandfather, you promised to go on with what you were telling us about Governor King,' said Fred

"Oh, I told you all about Governor King, I think boys, but I'll tell you about Governor McQuarrie[139].

Governor McQuarrie was a good man, and did a great deal for his country. At first the people disliked him because he called in all the papers that Governor King had made out – grants of land, free pardons, etc – and cancelled them all.

There was much excitement in Sydney – everybody expected to lose their all, and I don't know what they were going to do. But in a few days they had their papers returned to them – this time made out in Governor McQuarrie's name.

The Colonel who came out in Colonel Johnson's place was a great racing man. He brought out several horses and a jockey and two grooms. The Colonel's name was O'Connell, and he was very popular, being good hearted and open-handed. The Governor gave the regiment a piece of ground just outside the town for a racecourse. The soldiers turned out and stumped and levelled it, and made it as smooth as a table, and there they had the regimental races for a long time; but as the town grew, of course it didn't do to have the racecourse so near, so the ground was planted with trees and converted into a public garden known as the

---

[139] Major-General Lachlan Macquarie (b.1762 – d. 1824), Governor of New South Wales from 1810 to 1821. One of his first tasks was to arrest Colonel Johnson (see chapter 27) and re-establish order by reinstating officials sacked during the rebellion. He also cancelled the land and stock grants made prior to his arrival before officially re-issuing most of the grants again to avoid discontent.

Lover's Walk.   Last time I saw it, it was beautiful, and there were carriage drives winding through it.

Shortly after the McQuarrie's came to Sydney, my little brother's third birthday came round, and my mother put him in knickerbockers. In the afternoon Charlie rushed into the road to meet my father and show him a set of whistling bells that Lady King had sent him. Just as he reached the road Lady McQuarrie's carriage dashed round a corner. People shouted to the coachman, but he paid no heed, and before any of the onlookers could reach the child the foremost horse had knocked him down and two wheels passed over his body.

My father couldn't even pick up his own child – it was all he could do to protect the coachman, as the crowd were mobbing him. They would have killed him if they could; but my father told them they would be doing him the greatest kindness if they went away quietly, as he couldn't go while they were likely to molest the coachman, who, as it happens was drunk. So the people contented themselves by letting loose the horses and dragging the carriage to Government House[140].

Meanwhile Lady McQuarrie had picked Charlie up and carried him in to mother, who, when she saw him, fainted. And then I remember that the doctor came and said that death had been instantaneous, and a few days afterwards I remember going to the funeral and standing by the open grave holding my father's hand.

Years afterwards, when we lived in Hobart Town, Lady McQuarrie often came to see my mother, and she always used to cry and blame herself for my brother's death. She was a very good woman and most kind. Everybody liked her.

After Governor McQuarrie had been in Sydney about 18 months my father retired. He was coming into Sydney one night with despatches, when he was caught in a violent thunderstorm,  and he became stone deaf in one ear,  so he

---

[140] Williams little brother, Charles Thomas (b.10 Feb 1812 – d.6 October 1814) was killed by coachman Joseph Biggs. The inquest can be read in Historical Records of New South Wales (series 1, Vol. IX).

considered he would not be alert enough for this work after that. He had a good deal of property both in Sydney and Hobart Town; besides a large mob of cattle which Governor King had given him. As the Sydney property consisted of several town houses which my father let at good rents, we went down to Hobart Town to live. My father had nothing to do now, so being what is termed a horsey man, he went in largely for training.

When we first went to Hobart we lived in a house out near the gaol. The gaol had no wall round it then. Every morning some children used to go to the gaol with their little shovels and some she-oak embers would be given to them to start their fires with. One morning I was walking along with some of the little boys who came past our house, when we saw a man with a knapsack on his arm talking to some soldiers. We didn't take much notice of the man, but presently he walked after us, and asked if we'd like to see what he had in his knapsack. Of course we all crowded round thinking it was something funny. He knelt down on the road, opened the knapsack and to our horror lifted out a man's head by the hair! We all shrieked and ran, fire shovels and embers alike forgotten. I turned round and saw three soldiers rush at the man and cover him with their bayonets.

I heard afterwards it was the head of a man named Mike Howe[141], and the police had been out after him for a long time. This man had surprised him somehow, and had managed to take him, and was then on his way to Governor Sorrell to claim the reward.

"What was HIS name?" asked Jack

"Well, we didn't stop to inquire his name, Jack – we were all too frightened by what we saw and it was a ghastly sight to show children. Such a villainous looking face with eyes and mouth gaping open. The man who took him had several hundreds paid him and his passage to any port of the Queen's dominions.

---

[141] Notorious Tasmanian bushranger leader Michael Howe (b.1787 – d.1818) was involved in numerous robberies and shootouts. On 21 October 1818 he was tricked into a hut near the Shannon River where soldier William Pugh (48th regiment) and convict stock-keeper Thomas Worrall were lying in wait. All fired and missed, but during the struggle which followed Howe was killed by blows on the head with a musket.

He went to England, ran through his money, and was back in Australia again within three years of departing[142].

Soon after that we went to live in Collins Street, and much to my disgust I was sent to school. A Mr Fitzgerald kept the school, and he was harsh and cruel. Of course he had a lot to do – he had to teach boys of all sorts and conditions, ages and sizes, and he had to write the headings to all our copy books. But then again, we all used the same book – 'The Universal Spelling Book' – and all the punishment we received our parents took for granted we deserved. But nowadays, if a child hears the word 'stick,' he goes home and tells his parents, and they are up in arms in a minute, though I must own that sometimes we got a little too much from Mr Fitzgerald's stick.

Often the boys would have said their lessons all right, but they were too frightened and lost their wits completely. One morning I had a sound thrashing from him, and in the afternoon when I went up to say my spelling, I could hardly stand. I was only a very small boy, and there I stood quaking in front of him… I handed him the book and he glanced at it.

'Spell trot,' he thundered.

'T-r-o-t-t,' I stammered.

'I'll teach you to t-r-o-t-t, you young idiot!' he roared, and round and round the table and desks I ran, and he after me. The other boys were dying to laugh, but they daren't. At last he caught me, and I didn't feel much like laughing then, I can tell you.

One favourite mode of punishment he had was to stand the boys out at the door with a dunce's cap about two feet high on their heads, and a Bible in each hand, held straight out at arm's length. And it was punishment too. Everyone that passed in the street could see you and would laugh; and then again it was very

---

[142] It was probably Thomas Worrall that showed the children the head. He was granted a pardon and free passage to England by Sorrell. Private Pugh received £50 reward and Worrall's share was £45 (this roughly equates to a year's wage for a skilled craftsman of the time).

painful to keep your arms straight out for long; and every now and then he'd come sneaking out behind the boys, and if they had let down their arms they would get a crack that would send the books – and them too – flying.

One day I saw Mr Fitzgerald give a boy named Billy Mansfield a terrible thrashing, and he was as innocent as could be of what he was accused. Mrs Fitzgerald had been hunting round one day when she found a letter to a girl whose father kept a baker's shop, and Mrs F. declared that Billy had written the letter. In reality, the letter had been written by a hunchback called Johnny French, and we could all see that by the writing, and so could Mr Fitzgerald, but he wanted to thrash Billy, and thrash him he did.

Years afterwards Billy Mansfield and I went to Johnny French's funeral – he and his father were buried on the same day. They were the first to be buried in the Presbyterian Cemetery at Hobart Town."

Governor Macquarie and his wife Elizabeth, early 19th century. After Garran, 1888.

# Chapter 29

## *MY SCHOOLS AND SCHOOLMASTERS – JOCK PIPER'S EXPEDIENT –*
## *FROM SCHOOL TO SEA – ON BOARD A WHALER*

"Grandfather, please do go on telling us about when you were at school. I like hearing about that," said Jack.

"Yes Jack, it would do you good if you went to school like that for a little while; you wouldn't consider yourself so ill-used now, I can tell you. I wonder how any of you boys would like to be 'horsed' like we were?"

"What is being horsed?" we all asked.

"Why, being put on another boys back and being quilted[143] till we all roared with pain. If the boys were big, Mr Fitzgerald called in a man to hold them. One day a big boy, about 18, named Jock Piper, was horsed.

'Next time old Fitzgerald 'horses' me I'll bite the man's ears off,' said Jock.

And sure enough, about three weeks afterwards Jock Piper was to be 'horsed' again. In came the man Mr Fitzgerald always employed, and Jock mounted his willing steed. At the first stroke of the master's cane Jock made a snap at the man's ear and caught it between his teeth; then he wrapped his arms around the man's neck and clung to him like a leech. The man howled and ran all over the room, but Jock never loosed his hold till blood was streaming from the man's ear, and Jock let go then because he said he didn't want to be choked.

Soon after that the two boys in a front seat were playing a senseless game, which was always thought very exciting when we played it in school hours, and Mr Fitzgerald, glancing up from the sums he was setting, caught them in the act.

---

[143] Hit with a length of cane.

He intended to give them a good fright, so picking up a long black ruler, he threw it on the floor at the boy's feet, but it rebounded hitting one boy on the head, making him stone deaf. The boy never recovered his hearing and Mr Fitzgerald lost his billet.

The next man, Mr Stone, was even worse than his predecessor, and I for one, stayed away from school whenever I could possibly make an excuse – and often without making one.

My mother had died sometime before this, and my two sisters were at school, so I ran wild and did much as I liked. I rode a great deal, and knocked about stables with my father and other horsey men. It would not have been so bad if I had always kept with them, but I took to going about with the sailors and whalers who came to Hobart Town from time to time. Their conversation and customs were anything but what would tend to improve a boy. My father's friends, though they thought of little but horses, were never coarse and blasphemous, like the whalers often were, and I was at first often terrified at their language; but I soon got hardened to it.

Often I spent the time my father thought I spent in school with the whalers on the wharves and in the dockyards, till at last my one desire was to go whaling. I didn't say anything to my father about it. I could see he was disappointed that I thought less than he did of the horses.

Things went on in this fashion for some time, till one day I had really been to school and was playing marbles outside in the afternoon, when Captain Kelly[144] called me from the other side of the street and asked me if I would like to go whaling. Like to go! Why I nearly stood on my head with pride and excitement, and the captain, seeing my delight, patted me on the head and told me to go and ask my father, and if he consented, he would give me a berth.

I never went near my father, and was down on the wharf at the office almost as soon as Captain Kelly was. He, of course, thought I had permission to go. I went into the office and signed articles, and the captain gave me four dollars advance and the 70$^{th}$ lay.

---

[144] Captain James Kelly (b.1791–d.1859), the "Father and Founder of Whaling in Tasmania".

I don't know exactly how I spent that night for we didn't start till morning. I often thought in those long hours when I was waiting for the day to dawn what my father would say when he heard what I had done, I thought with some uneasiness how good he had been to me. I always had money and horses and everything I had wanted, and yet I was doing what I distinctly knew he would not have allowed.

When morning came we started in a small schooner, and towed a whaleboat behind. There were only two of us going to our party – the rest were down at the station. When we arrived there I found that we knew a good many of the hands, and was quite happy. I could both pull and swim well, and was a favourite with the men, so I had rather a good time of it than otherwise.

My father didn't miss me for a little. We led a free and easy Bohemian life, and I often spent a night with one or other of father's friends. But when he did miss me he thought I was drowned. I, with some other mischievous boys, used to get into a boat belonging to an old man who brought butter and milk to Hobart Town. The minute he got safely off with his butter and things, we'd jump in and pull about as long as we thought it safe. If the old man could catch us, as he sometimes did, he'd throw us all into the water. Most of us could swim like ducks, and it did us no harm.

However someone had told my father that he'd seen me going away in a whaler. My father ascertained the truth from Captain Kelly and that he worried terribly about me, and blamed himself for not looking after me more.

I remember when I came home again in about four months[145] my father looked a great deal older, and what he said to me hurt me more than volumes of reproach;

'Thank God your mother isn't alive, my boy,' he said, 'If she had been you would have broken her heart.'"

---

[145] The *Colonial Times and Tasmanian Advertiser* (2 September 1825, p.2) reported that Captain Kelly's schooner the *Australian* arrived in port from the River Derwent whaling station. In total they caught 16 whales and netted some 150 tuns of oil and 6 tons of whalebone.

Captain Kelly, c.1830s. Courtesy K. Bowden.

# Chapter 30

*MY FIRST WHALE – THE IMPERIAL MEASURE – WHALERS ASHORE –*

*AN OLD TIME RACE MEETING – A SCURVY TRICK*

"Grandfather you haven't told us anything about your first whaling season," said Fred

"Have I not my boy? Well, I'm afraid there's nothing much to tell – at least nothing much to my credit. I was only young you must remember, and not a particularly wise boy either.

I'll never forget the first whale we fastened to... I was scared and it was enough to scare a much older person than I was too. I was in Catlin's boat – the same man that Catlin's River is named after[146] – and soon after we had fastened to the whale it came to a sudden stop, the line was not very long and before we knew what was happening, the boat's nose was right over the whale's head. I was seriously thinking of jumping overboard then, but a man named Makin bawled to me to sit still. The whale was spouting water and blood all over us, and I can assure you it was anything but pleasant, and I thought to myself, if this is whaling, I don't think much of it!

The next time we fastened to a whale, I didn't mind so much, but it didn't seem so glorious as I thought while on there.

We were whaling in Adventure Bay[147] that season, and I was holding a piece of the horse flesh for Chamberlain one night when he was mincing the blubber. We were at it all night, and just at day dawn Chamberlain gave me a bucket and told me to go to a well and get some water to make tea with.

---

[146] Captain Catlin's name now also refers to the Catlins area, the rugged south-east corner of the South Island, partially in both Southland and Otago.

[147] At Bruny Island, Tasmania.

Off I went willing enough, but when I stooped down to fill the bucket I heard a sound that nearly froze my blood. A strange pattering noise it was, and it seemed to come from the well too. I was frightened to look up almost, but at last I raised my head and looked all round, but in the semi-darkness nothing but the trees were visible. Still the noise went on, and I believe I was more scared than ever.

Somehow (I don't know to this day how I managed it) I stumbled back to where the others were, and told Chamberlain that I was sure there was an evil spirit or something in the water. Laugh! How they all laughed at me, I'll never forget.

'Why you young fool, it was only a kangaroo,' said Chamberlain. However he saw that I was genuinely frightened, and sent someone else for the water. I heard him tell the men 'not to be rough on the kid – he's so beastly young yet.'

Well after the season was over we went back to Hobart Town, and what a terrible bobbery[148] there was too, among the whalers.

It was the season the Imperial measure was introduced, and it took exactly one-fifth more oil to make a tun than formerly. Then again we had signed articles to the effect that we were to be paid in dollars – a dollar going for five shillings currency.

We were paid accordingly to that, but when we came to use our money a dollar was only worth four shillings sterling. A good number of men were furious and refused to take their money, declaring that it was downright robbery. So they were told to take the oil then, but those of them who were able to get casks found that the merchants would not give anymore for the oil than the owners would, so they had just to take what they got and be thankful.

It didn't really matter to me. Although I was only on the '70th lay', I got a good deal of money. My father was so hurt and angry at my conduct that he refused to touch my money, so I squandered it as I liked.

---

[148] *Bobbery* = a noisy commotion.

It was the worst thing that could have happened to me, for I formed the habit, which was the ruin of so many whalers, living like a fighting cock so long as my money lasted, and then – and not till then – going back to hard work.

Now that we were in town again, of course we determined to have plenty. I thought it was splendid to swagger about familiarly with men three times my age. Some of them were right-down good fellows, and straight as a die too; but others again were anything but desirable.

We reached Hobart Town just before the annual races, and of course we all attended. That year a chap named Bob Jillet rode an extraordinary race. He was only about 18, and the best rough rider about Hobart Town[149].

The course in Hobart Town then was in the shape of a complete circle and was three miles round. This particular race was to be run in three heats, of one round each, with a spell of some minutes between each heat. There were nine horses to start, and as the starter gave signal, *Saladin* (Bob's horse) made a tremendous bound forward, and both girths snapped, but Bob sat firm as could be, put his whip in his mouth and rode round with the rest. The owner of *Saladin* was standing by on another horse when he saw the start and the girths flying and flapping round the horse's legs. He rode after Jillet as fast as he could.

'Pull up boy, you'll be killed man,' but Bob never heeded him – he either couldn't or wouldn't pull up.

Round they flew. Bob was a bit behind however, and only just saved his distance, otherwise he'd have been out of the running in the next two heats. They found, on examining the girths that they had been burnt through with vitriol. It was a dirty trick and might have cost Jillet his life.

---

[149] Robert 'Bob' Jillet was the first son born to Robert Jillet Snr. and Elizabeth Bradshaw. In many ways the lives of Bob and William took similar paths: both their families were Hobart based, both were 'horsey' people; both men inherited substantial properties in Australia but forsook the life of a landlord for adventures in New Zealand whaling fisheries. Jillet Station on Kapiti Island (home of Te Rauparaha) was founded by his family. The well respected Captain Wiliam Young (mentioned in chapter 31), was also Bob Jillet's brother-in-law (*pers. comm.* Kris Herron, descendant of the Jillet family, 2011).

Next two heats he came in flying, and didn't he get cheered! The people in the grandstand collected a large sum of money for him and gave it to his mother.

'I won't see a penny of that,' said Bob as he was passing by to be weighed out. 'It's very kind of them to go investing my money in the Sinking Fund.'

But poor Bob, when he got into the scale he was so light-hearted because of his success, that he was underweight. His master struck him angrily with his whip.

'D___ you Bob,' he said, 'You've lost the race. I'm a ruined man.'

The scales went down in a minute and stayed down too. Poor Bob was so disappointed he was nearly in tears.

'It's all right,' said the clerk kindly, 'You've won after all. Your weight's all right, and you deserve to win too.'

Bob jumped off and was all smiles again in a moment. Everybody wanted to shake hands with him, and his master couldn't say enough in his praise."

# Chapter 31

### *WHALING EPISODES – A NARROW ESCAPE – THE FIRST OF JUNE –*

### *GETTING RID OF PROPERTY – SEQUEL TO A MORTGAGE*

"Grandfather, tell us a yarn tonight please. Go on telling us about when you were whaling as a boy," said Fred

"Well boys, the second year I pulled the after-oar in Sharp's boat. We were whaling for a Mr Meredith at Oyster Bay. We had a very bad season though – our boat never took a single whale. Sharp, the headsman, was a very old man, though a good hand, but the steerer was a very poor chap in the boat. We were right on a fine big whale one day, but the boat steerer let her off somehow. For every whale that was caught Mr Meredith gave the hands three extra gallons of rum. It was vile stuff, I thought, and I used to sell all mine to the headsman, who gave me everything he had for a drop of grog.

Next year in '28 I think it would be, I pulled the after-oar in Griffiths' boat. We were then whaling for Young and Walford[150] at Hull Bay. I remember that year very well. Young was with us down at the fishery – a fine young fellow he was then too, just 28 – born with the century he used to say. He was the best fellow out to command a fishery. None of the whalers ever tried their little games twice on him.

We had a splendid season that year. One day we caught three whales, and in the afternoon I was given charge of our boat to pull in and get a new line. There were four men with me, and when we got in to the station, we found that Mr Walford,

---

[150] Captains William Young and Bernard Walford. Captain Young's obituary supports William Thomas' high regard: *"A GOOD man in every respect. An able colonist, a farmer who could plough, reap and sow. A Mariner, that could sail a ship to any part of the world, a whaler, whose exploits are unequalled in the annals of daring a Tasmanian in heart and soul, a loving husband, and a good father; and to sum up all - AN HONEST MAN. Mark his career, sons of Tasmania, and emulate his enterprise and his virtues."*

our other owner, had arrived. Two watermen had brought him in their boat from town.

He was a fast young man, rather given to gambling, and not nearly so well liked by all of us as Mr Young was. Well this day he brought with him ten gallons of very strong rum to treat all hands. He told me to fetch him a quart pot, which he filled and told me to take out in the boat.

In twenty minutes two of the men were dead drunk – could neither sit, stand nor go. I was in a hurry to get out again, as it was getting late and they wanted the line to tow the whales in. The other two men didn't drink, so they were all right. We dragged the two fellows who were speechless drunk into a safe place, and took the two watermen (Tom Myers and Major Lee) in their places.

When we got out Mr Young thought the other two men had run away. I never said anything about it, and he was too busy to ask me, but when we got in he was awfully angry, and pitched into Walford at a great rate for making such beasts of the men.

We were all wet and cold and hungry, and went in to our supper; but lo and behold, there was no supper. The cook was on the floor drunk. Mr Young was furious and gave old Bobby Manders a terrible shake – he had been in the Young family for years. He looked around with senseless drunken eyes. 'Never mind Bill, my boy,' said he, 'it's the first of June. Lord Howe defeated the Dutch. It's a day for England to be proud of.'[151]

'Yes and you are a pig for England to be proud of. Get up and get some supper,' said Young.

'Oh but never mind supper,' repeated Bobby, 'It's the Glorious First of June!' and that's all we could get out of him. We had to get supper the best way we could and light our own fire. It happened that it really was the first of June, and I think I remember that history lesson better than any Mr Fitzgerald taught me.

---

[151] The Glorious First of June (1794), celebrating when the British fleet engaged and beat the French fleet in the Atlantic.

Next year we whaled in Trumpeter Bay for the same owners. I was just 18 then, and was made a boat steerer. I was reckoned a smart chap for my age, and I thought so myself too. As I was young they thought it would cause dissatisfaction if I had the ordinary lay, so they gave me the 30$^{th}$ lay, but Mr Young was always giving me presents, which more than made up for it. Trumpeter Bay was splendid place, and we had a grand season. Though we only had two boats, we got a tremendous lot of oil.

That was the year that Governor Arthur allowed liquor to go into the fisheries duty free. In some of the fisheries a terrible lot of drinking went on, but they didn't drink much in our fishery – no man ever got drunk twice there. Trumpeter Bay was a very bad place for a vessel to lie. Whenever it blew a strong sou'-wester she had to run up to town, but she always came down again for us to cut in our whales at. Next year I was boat-steerer again for the same owners, but this time in Adventure Bay. We did very well there too. One afternoon we were cutting in a whale. I was standing on the whale, and they were just hoisting up a piece of blubber about four feet wide, 25 or 30 feet long, and weighing between two and three tons. It was going up all right, when all of a sudden it carried away the fall and down it came, blocks and all. A lot of the men swore that they saw it strike me, but it didn't. It must have struck the whale and turned it over so quickly that I was in the water before I was struck. We were lying in four or five fathoms of water, and I know I went right to the bottom. I came up again all right and hung on to the bobstay. They were looking all round for me, and when one man saw me there, he jumped overboard to save me. However he couldn't swim very well so I was better off than he was, because I was more used to being in the water.

They wouldn't believe me that I was unhurt, and insisted on my going up to the fishery and going to bed. I didn't object of course, and got the cook to give me a rare feed, which in those days was a panacea for all my woes. I went to sleep for a bit, and when the others came in I heard Griffiths, our headsman tell the others not to disturb me. I was wide awake and as right as could be, but I thought I'd play the invalid. Next morning Griffiths said to me,

'Are you better boy?'

'Yes thanks,' I said, 'I am as well as I always am. It didn't do me a bit of harm.'

He could hardly believe it. He thought I'd be half dead.

'I'm very sorry for you my boy,' said Griffiths, 'I've got bad news for you. A man came down about ten last night and said that your father is dead. We didn't like to tell you till this morning. Young has been worrying all night, thinking that perhaps you would have to be buried with your father.'

There was no fear of that, but I was awfully cut up about my father. I went up to town at once. Mr Young insisted on coming with me, and he gave me a suit of mourning clothes. Both my sisters were well off and married, so I got most of my father's property. But I didn't want it. I gave most of it to them; they didn't want to take it, but I made them. I made ducks and drakes of the rest pretty soon, for I never cared or thought about saving money. One section I mortgaged for £20. I never paid anything on it, and afterwards the man I mortgaged it to sold it for as many thousands."

# Chapter 32

*MORE ABOUT WHALING – MR GELLIBRAND'S RIGHTS – UNJUST LAWS –*

*HOW THEY WERE RIGHTED*

"Grandfather, please go on telling us about whaling,' said Jack.

"Yes my boy, if you like," said Grandfather, "Let me see, I think I told you about my poor father's death last time. Well, I stayed in town three days for the funeral, and then went back to Trumpeter Bay till the end of the season.

And a good season it was too, but towards the end a spell of bad weather set in and we ran up to town for a few days. One day there was a strong S.E. gale blowing, and a whale came right up among the shipping.

Mr Young and some of us went out in a boat, and fastened to and killed the whale, then anchored it down at the South Arm, intending to go and cut it in the first fine day. Next day was fairly good, and we started out with our vessel to cut in the whale, but someone had been there before us, for on going up to the whale we saw in large letters, 'Mr Mortimer: his property.'

Mortimer had gone past early in the morning in his boat, and seeing the whale, as he though unanchored, claimed it as his own.

'I'll property the wretch,' said Mr Young; and when they came up presently; there was a row, but Young proved that the whale was his and we proceeded to cut her in.

I was sent ashore with two other fellows to get some ballast. We went in a large whaleboat, and soon got on board about a ton of ballast, and were pulling back to the vessel when I saw what I thought was a woman running down the beach and beckoning to us. I told the others, and they turned round to have a look.

'It's Mr Gellibrand[152]; we'd better go back,' said one of the men. Mr Gellibrand was a great man then. His son had come out as Attorney-General to Judge Pedder, and he himself had a lot of property. We pulled ashore, and there stood the old man in his dressing gown.

'My good men,' he said, 'who authorised you to take away my stones?'

'Mr Young did,' I said, 'We want ballast before we can cut in our whale out there.'

'Well,' he said, 'Mr Young had no right to do that. Why, if everybody came and helped themselves to my stones, I'd soon not have one on my beach. Unload your boat, my good men.'

'But,' I said, 'I thought anyone had a right to stones below high water mark?'

'No,' he said, 'my grant gives me the stones right down to low water mark, so again I request you to unload.'

Of course we had nothing to do now but unload, and we flung the stone over with as much force as we could, and splashed the old fellow properly.

'I wonder if he'd like a little of MY water,' whispered one of the men to me, and angry as I was, I couldn't help laughing. But the old gentleman stood his ground well and saw every stone out.

When we were pulling back to the ship he told me to tell Mr Young to come ashore to him at once. When we reached the vessel Mr Young was terribly angry, but I explained to him. He flung himself into a boat and we went ashore again.

Mr Gellibrand harangued there for about an hour, and at last he wound up by saying;

'Now Mr Young, you are welcome to any quality of ballast at any time. That's where I live,' pointing to his house, 'and it's very easy for you to come and ask me when you want any.'

---

[152] William Gellibrand (b.1765 – d. 1840), founded and operated the Tasmanian Bank with his son, Joseph Tice Gellibrand.

Young couldn't say anything to him, but when he got away he did rave.

'That old Tomfoolery in petticoats is very fond of asserting his authority, but if I were to contest it in a court of law, I don't think he'd look quite so smart,' he said, and he was angry for the rest of the day.

Next season we were in Trumpeter Bay again, and had a splendid season – there were plenty of whales everywhere then. Though we only had two boats, we got 300 tuns of oil; of course we had to work hard for it.

Next year (1830) Young and Walford had two fisheries – one in Adventure Bay and one in Trumpeter Bay. I was boat-steerer in Griffiths' boat and we went into either fishery – which ever happened to be handiest – after the day's work was over. One afternoon we were ashore in Adventure Bay. Griffiths went up to the look-out point, and saw Young's boat and a strange boat out with three whales.

He came down and told us to get ready to go out; so off we went, both boat loads of us. When we got out, there was a great row going on. Young had fastened to a whale which however, broke the iron and got away. Then the other boat, belonging to a man named Lucas; fastened to it and there they were arguing away about the ownership of the whale.

While they were in the thick of it the whale got away again, and so we gave chase and fastened on to the self-same whale.

Then somehow, either the fast whale or the loose whale – it all happened so quickly we never knew which – flew through the water right on top of us, and stove in our boat. We were all sent flying into the water, but none of us were hurt. We managed to right our boat and were towed ashore by our other boat.

For the third time, then, the poor whale got away; but Young and Lucas both went after it, and both headsmen fastened to it at the same time, and they commenced quarrelling again. By this time it was getting a bit dark and was time to go in, so both of them insisted on putting his own line and anchor to the whale and leaving it till the morning; and Young declared that however early Lucas's boat was there in the morning he'd be there as soon.

And sure enough, he was there at daylight, though he had come all the way from Trumpeter Bay; and they commenced fighting about the whale again. Young proved, however, that by the existing whaling rules the whale was his, and Lucas had to give in.

About that time there was so much quarrelling and so many petty court cases between the different whalers and owners that the authorities determined to find out for themselves how whaling was conducted in the fisheries. So Judge Montagu came down to Trumpeter bay and lived there all the season in his yacht. Every morning he went out in our boat, and he was always asking questions about the rules we had, and the life we led.

Of course the whaling rules had been laid down by men who knew nothing whatsoever about the sea, and some of them were unjust. For instance, if one boat fastened to and killed a calf, they could claim the mother too, even if another boat had taken her a few yards off. Then again, if a whale your iron was in got away and another boat fastened to her days afterwards, you could claim the whale though you had no hand in killing her.

After Judge Montagu had been down there, all that was altered, and far fairer whaling laws were enforced."

# Chapter 33

*WHALING ADVENTURES – AT CLOSE QUARTERS WITH A SHARK –*

*THE LATE CAPTAIN HOWELL – A GRAND OLD PIONEER –*

*THE LOSS OF THE AMAZON*

"Grandfather, will you tell us what a boat steerer had to do – what his work was, I mean," said Fred.

"Well my boy, a boatsteerer's work was not very easy, and rather risky too, unless a person was nimble and could balance himself well; but of course, as in most things, use went a long way. The boat steerer pulls the foremost oar (the harp'ner oar, they call it) till the headsman gives the order to lance; then he goes for'ard and stands in the bow with the iron raised in his hand till the moment comes to let the iron fly. Then he pays the rope out. The box-lining coil, as it is called, is fastened to the harpoon, and lies in the bow of the boat; the other end runs aft, and is fastened to the loggerhead. Then after the whale is fastened to, the boatsteerer steers for the headsman after the whale, and that is the hardest part of all – at least I used to think so.

I remember will one afternoon we were out, both our boat and Young's, and we fastened to a whale. We had seen three whales coming in from seaward, and that was why went out, though it was rough. Young's boat was about a mile and a half from our boat, when Bill Gully, the boatsteerer said to Young;

'Griffiths' boat has gone down, I saw it.'

'Gone down!' said Young, 'Rubbish! They've lowered the sail, that's all.'

'A sail doesn't go down like that when it's lowered,' persisted Gully, so Young told them to pull in our direction. Gully was right too. The line fastened to the whale was too short, and as we were towing along she sank, taking down the boat with her. We were all in the water in a minute.

Four of the men started at once to swim to seaward towards Young's boat, and I was just going with them when an Australian native named George Chase, who pulled the after oar, called out to me:

'Oh Bill, for God's sake don't leave me!'

I had quite forgotten about the poor chap, and he couldn't swim either. I couldn't leave him like that so I swam back to him with another oar. He had kept hold of his own oar all the time. I put an oar under each arm, and was surprised how splendidly he floated.

We hadn't been long there when I felt the rough back of a shark against my feet. I pulled off my coat, which was a rough pilot, determined to do all I could to save my life; but I needn't have troubled myself, for the shark went down to the whale and didn't think any more about us. When Young's boat came up I was eating a piece of fat damper which floated near me, and they did chaff me. One fellow began singing:

*'Some fell on their bended knees,*

*And others fell to weeping;*

*But I fell to my bread and cheese,*

*For I always look out for the main thing!'*

Years afterwards in Otago, the chaps used to chaff me about that fat damper, and Billy Gully would sing that same Irish song that they sang that day. It was the signal for a volley of chaff for me.

That same day though, Griffiths', our headsman, was nearly drowned. He depended rather too much on his swimming powers, and didn't stop to take off any of his clothes, but started off with boots, coat, sou'wester, and two pairs of trousers on. Of course that hampered him terribly, and he was just at his last gasp when they hauled him into the boat.

That same season Griffiths was nearly killed too. One day our two boats were out after three whales, and we had each fastened to one, when I saw the loose whale coming right underneath our boat. I called out to Griffiths, and he turned to me and bawled out:

'Damn you and the loose whale too – attend the boat!'

Scarcely were the words out of his mouth when the loose whale turned round and struck Griffiths with the corner of her flukes and sent him flying aft against the anchor. His head was terribly cut, and he lay there motionless, with blood streaming from the wound in his head.

We all thought he was dead, and the men were saying it was a judgement on him, for the whale did not touch the boat – never struck a man but Griffiths, though it might have settled us all. I felt wild with them though, because a few minutes before they all had been indulging in language a good deal worse.

He lay there a good while, till a chap we always called Old Harry saw him move, so he emptied the fresh water keg over him, and then we saw some signs of returning life. We left Young to anchor the three whales, for they got the other one, and we pulled in with Dick Griffiths and put him to bed. He was delirious for three days, but the cook kept dosing him with tea and rum – always with the same comforting remark that:

'If it doesn't do him any good, it can't do him any harm.'

A few mornings afterwards Young came out of the hut and said to me

'Well it had been RUM treatment, but it has answered all right, for Griffiths is himself again.'"

"Grandfather," said Fred, as there was a considerable pause after he finished about Griffiths, "Could you tell us who brought the first cattle and sheep here[153]? A fellow was asking me the other day if you knew."

---

[153] To Invercargill.

"Well I don't know who brought them here my boy, but I know that Captain Howell brought the first cattle (about 80 head) to Riverton in the *Kairari*. He brought them from Twofold Bay[154], also a mare and a foal. He gave all of his relations so many head of cattle each, on the condition that he got the male increase for a certain time for beef for his vessel.

Then some years afterwards, when he came down from Sydney in the *Eliza*, he brought between 500 and 600 sheep and shared them with his relations. He was about the best man to his own people I ever saw. The reason he brought the *Eliza* was because he lost his vessel, the *Amazon*. One dark, thick, rainy night they were coming from Jacob's River to the Bluff. Tommy Chasland remarked that it wasn't fit to go into the Bluff, but they all chaffed him and said that he wanted to go to Stewart Island because his wife was there, so when they shaped her head into the Bluff, Tommy went below.

They hadn't gone far before the vessel ran on to the rocks at the Point. If they had put Tommy in charge that would not have happened. Well they couldn't manage the vessel off the rocks so they resolved to wait till morning and float her on the flood tide. But by daybreak there wasn't a spar of the *Amazon* to be seen.

But it didn't affect Captain Howell much – he was worth thousands then. He brought the *Frolic* from Johnny Jones, paying for it in oil. Then he filled her with oil and took her to Sydney. He sold the oil well, and the *Frolic* too, though she wasn't worth much and as rotten as a pear. She was built of what we call apple-tree. Then he bought the *Eliza* and came back to Jacob's River. He brought the sheep with him and 1500 sovereigns tied up in a dirty old silk handkerchief. I remember seeing it handed to him over the vessel's side into the boat."

"Grandfather, you promised to tell us about Judge Montagu," said Jack.

"So I did," answered Grandfather, "but we'll have to put that off for another time now."

---

[154] On the south coast of New South Wales.

# Chapter 34

*GRANDFATHER'S RING – HOW HE GOT IT –*

*BISHOP SELWYN AT STEWART ISLAND – A MUCH USED KEEPSAKE.*

"Grandfather, where did you get your ring?" asked Fred this afternoon. Fred was always inquisitive.

"My poor old ring; there's not much of it left now Fred, but I'll tell you it's history if you like," said Grandfather

"We have to go a long way back to when I was a young fellow whaling in Avalon[155]. I was considered a good sort of a chap then – but that's neither here nor there. Well one afternoon we were 'trying out'[156], when we heard a woman yelling and screaming;

*'Murder!'*

We knew who it was all right. It was the wife of the owner of another fishery a little way from ours. The man was a brute and often thrashed his wife, and we thought her cries were perhaps overrated, and anyway I didn't like to interfere. Presently an old Irish whaler, named Andy Moore, came up and asked if I knew the consequences of hearing murder called out. But we were very busy at the time and I only grunted.

'Be jabbers,' he said, 'it's no laughing matter. If you don't go to that woman's assistance I'll count you as bad as her husband.' So we both took our spades and ran to the fellow's hut. We didn't wait to knock, but just opened the door and walked in.

---

[155] The whaling settlement Avalon is now a beachside suburb north of Sydney.

[156] *Trying down* = boiling down whale blubber in huge iron pots.

We felt a bit sick at the sight we saw and poor impulsive Irish Andy went as white as a sheet and began rubbing his eyes. The woman stood there with hardly any clothing on, her long brown hair streaming all around her, with blood pouring from a wound on her head.

It was really a terrible sight, and I asked the man what he meant, and he told me to mind my own business. I told him if he wasn't careful everyone in the settlement would be at the hut in a minute, there was such a row going on. He was about three times drunk, but the coward had enough sense left to see that it wouldn't be good for him if all the men came in.

He called his little girl and asked her what her mother had been doing while he was away.

'Mother went to the store, Dad, and took some rum out of a bottle and drank it.'

'Holy mother!' said Andy, 'the child's so frightened of ye that she's just lying to plaze ye. YE BRUTE!' and Andy was just about right too.

Anyway, we saved that woman from any more ill-usage, and soon afterwards she left her husband. I told her before that if it hadn't been for Andy I wouldn't have interfered, so she ought to have thanked him for it, but she didn't. You see, I was young and good-looking then boys, and she was beautiful, she wasn't like any other woman there. But she was tied to another man, and so we parted.

A few years afterwards, Old Jock bought me this little ring from HER. It was her wedding ring, and she was dead, poor soul.

Well time went on. I always kept the ring till in '44, when we were living at the Neck, when Bishop Selwyn[157] arrived. The Bishop had come over to Horseshoe in Bloody Jack's schooner, and was the object of a great deal of interest, and I must say amusement too. The Maori children were all in fits at his apron. He gave us each a card with his name and Lord Bishop of New Zealand on it, and weren't

---

[157] Bishop George Augustus Selwyn (b.1809 – d.1878), the first Anglican bishop of New Zealand.

those cards treasured by the natives.

Well, we had a service – not that that was altogether unusual, for Captain Anglem read prayers sometimes – and then the Bishop asked if any of us wanted to be married. Captain Anglem was wild.

'I am married,' he said, 'by the law of this country, and that's as binding in the sight of God as all the parsons in the world could make it.'

'I quite agree with you,' said the Bishop, 'but now you have a chance of marrying according to the customs of your own country, are you willing to avail yourself of it?'

'O, certainly,' said Captain Anglem.

So we were all married. I went first, because the ring belonged to me. It was the only ring there was then, and fifteen couples were married with it. I believe I'm the only one alive that was married that day. I can't remember who they all were now, but there was Jack Foster, Carter, Lowrie, Hunter, Gomez (Gooms), Jacky Lee, Stuart, Cooper, Captain Anglem, and a good many others. I can't think of their names, but there were fifteen of us altogether.

After it was over, the Bishop made us promise to be true to the church, and not listen to the 'krakia' of any Dissenters[158]. He promised to send a Church of England missionary to teach the children and hold services, and asked us to see that he never wanted for food or anything. Well, we promised, but he never sent the missionary, and in '51 – seven years afterwards – when he came back the old Maoris did go for him.

When old Pitu saw him coming up the beach, he called out – 'Oh Pihopa, Pihopa, tongata parau' (Bishop, Bishop, you told a lie). Then the Bishop said he didn't send a man because Mr Honere had come there, but that would not satisfy the Maoris, because he had told them not to listen to any but Church clergymen."

---

[158] Selwyn is referring to the karakia (prayers) of the 'heathen' Maori priests.

"Grandfather, may I use your ring when I get married?" said Jack

"Certainly you may my boy, but I hope for your wife's sake it won't be for a long time. She'll be the seventeenth woman who has been married with that ring."

"When Jack gets married! Well, I like that," said Fred, "I hope he'll have got over carrying worms and stick-jaw and Lindsay Gordon[159] all in the one pocket before then."

Bishop Selwyn c.1840s. Unknown artist.

---

[159] Lindsay Gordon (1833-1870) was a well known Australian poet, jockey, and politician.

# Chapter 35

*OLD WHALING DAYS – JUDGE MONTAGU –*

*GEORGE "THE BUTCHER" – THE JUDGE'S "AT HOME"*

"Grandfather, now tell us tonight about Judge Montagu[160], will you please?"

"Well boys, I think I've told you almost all there is to tell. In '31 he was down in our fishery overlooking the whaling laws, or 'whalings,' as we used to call them.

After he went back to Hobart-town things were a bit altered for the whalers; but it think I told you before about the quarrelling they used to go in for. The Judge came down to the fishery in his yacht, which we hauled high up, and there lived all the time. Every day he came out in our boat and took an interest in us all; so of course we all liked him.

I was boat steerer then, and he thought me a smart boy, for I was very young. There was a fellow in our boat named George Newman, whom we all called 'the Butcher'. This fellow amused the Judge very much, for he had a great appetite. One day the Judge saw him with a tremendous piece of Irish pork and a huge chunk of damper. He asked Mr Young if 'the Butcher' would get through all that.

'Oh yes, easily,' said Mr Young.

And every day after that the Judge would give us the remains of his lunch, and didn't 'the Butcher' enjoy it too – the Judge's dainty ham and chicken.

One day we were out on Monaku Bluff, and the Judge said to 'the Butcher' and me that whenever we came to town we must promise to go to his house and see him. We promised and we did go when we went up to town one day with a load of oil, and to take down a fresh cargo of casks.

---

[160] Judge Algernon Sidney Montagu (1802 – d. 1880). He lived on the east side of the Derwent River, near the present Hobart suburb of Montagu Bay.

We had been working hard all day, and were as greasy and dirty as possibly, when all of a sudden 'the Butcher' said to me:

'Let's go and see the Judge.'

So we went, dirty and all as we were. The Judge lived in a large house that stood in ground of his own – very extensive and beautifully kept. We tried the gate, but it was locked, so I jumped over the fence, and 'the Butcher' was just following me when up came an orderly and grabbing me by the shoulder, asked my business.

I shook myself free and told him I had come to see the Judge. He wanted to know rather much, and was pumping me, and said he didn't think the Judge would see us at this time of night. I said to him:

'You go and tell the Judge that two whalers – 'Young Billy' and 'the Butcher' – want to see him, and then see if he'll receive us at this time of night or not.'

In went the chap and in a few minute the Judge himself came out and greeted us most cordially, much to the astonishment and evident disgust of the watchman. The Judge Montagu took us into his drawing-room in all our filth. It was so warm and luxurious, and the chairs looked so dainty, that I was ashamed to sit down, for we were as greasy as horse-pieces, and not so pleasantly odorous either.

There were a lot of the Judge's friends in there too, and that made me worse than ever. He introduced us to them all, and made such a fuss over us, his friends looked a bit astonished. Then he questioned us about all our doings and takings, and kept us talking there for over two hours.

We had to go then to get back to our ship before she sailed. I often saw the Judge afterwards in Hobart-town. He was a splendid fellow. All the whalers in our fishery thought the world of him.

# Chapter 36

*BILLY MANSFIELD – HIS ADVENTURES AFLOAT AND ASHORE –*

*THE COURSE OF TRUE LOVE ETC*

"Grandfather, please tell us a yarn tonight," said Fred.

"Well my boy, what shall I tell you about? I was thinking tonight about an old school-fellow of mine named Billy Mansfield, I think I have spoken of him before to you haven't I?"

"Yes," said Jack, "I remember he was the chap who was blamed for writing a letter which he never saw in his life before, wasn't he?"

"Yes," said Grandfather, "that's poor old Billy. He was as decent a chap as ever I saw. We were mates for years until I came down here and lost sight of him altogether. Billy's father was the pilot in Hobart Town in those days; he was a nice man, a gentleman by birth, but he was rather too fond of frequenting hotels and shouting for everybody, and he mixed up with people a good deal above him in position, and it cost him something to entertain them in the same manner as they entertained him; so the family were kept on pretty short commons.

When Billy grew up and went whaling, his father calmly put down all his accounts to Billy. I know he kept his mother and sister too; they lived on a farm close to The Passage. I remember the first thing Billy always did when he came to town was to go around to all the hotels and pay his father's bills.

I don't believe a better son and brother ever lived than poor Billy; but for all that he was a great one for larking and getting into scrapes; he was what you boys would call in your latter day slang, a hard case, but he was straight for all that, and very good hearted too.

Well, after a time Captain Lovett asked Mr Mansfield to let Billy go to New Zealand with him, so Billy had to go, as his father wanted him to learn navigation. Captain Lovett was well known as a tyrant[161], but he didn't ill-use Billy, for he knew if he did so, when he returned to Hobart Town the boys would mob him, as Billy was born in Hobart Town. I came down here first with the same captain, and for the same reason he never ill-used me. But he was an old Tory all the same. Sam Lindsay, his chief mate on one voyage, he ordered, for no apparent reason, to the main rigging in a fearful storm, and made him look to wind'ard for hours, with the rain and sleet beating on him all the time, and the wind almost carrying him away.

When Billy left the ship the Captain asked him if he could recommend anyone to go in his place, and Billy recommended Jack Howell (afterwards Captain Howell), and so he came down to New Zealand with him.

One afternoon Jack Howell was rafting water to the ship from a small island called Marna[162]. Somehow his rafting did not please Captain Lovett and he jumped into the water, came up to Howell and hit him in the face.

Howell flew into a terrible passion and catching the unfortunate captain by the scruff of the neck, he almost drowned him. He told me he believed he would have finished the captain altogether only that Mrs Lovett caught sight of him through the cabin window and called out,

'Oh Mr Howell, for God's sake, don't drown my poor husband.'

But to return to Billy Mansfield, was whaling with Bill and Jack Sherbert down in Southport.

Billy was engaged then to a girl named Mona Stanfield. She was then at a boarding school in Hobart Town and her people lived at Kangaroo Point.

---

[161] See chapter 3.

[162] Mana Island is about 3km offshore from Porirua Harbour, near Wellington.

Poor Billy was very hard hit and whenever she sent him word that she would be away from school for a few days, or whatever it was, he would tip some of the men to row him up to Hobart Town from South Port – a distance of 60 miles. They would generally start after dark, about dusk, and row through the night.

They were terribly in love those two, and such a contrast too: she was a gentle, refined, beautiful sort of a girl, whilst he was a great rollicking jolly sailor; but rough and all as he was, she loved him, and was as proud of his whaling exploits as if he had been an Admiral commanding a line of battle.

But poor Billy always seemed to be getting into hot water. I remember once we were at a place – not a very desirable place certainly – when something riled Billy, and he and some other man began fighting; they went at it hammer and tongs for a while, and Billy gave the fellow an awful licking.

At last when it was over, someone asked Billy if he knew who he had been fighting with.

'No,' said Billy, 'and what's more I don't care.'

Then they told him it was a great pugilist[163] that was going round then, but as we were not often in town then we didn't know anything about the man. Billy put on his coat and pretended to be awfully frightened.

Well this Miss Mona's father must have heard somehow of this scene, and the very next day we were on the wharf and Billy was larking with some of the whalers, when who should come along but Mr Stanfield.

Now Mr Stanfield was a man of the grand old English gentleman order, and of course was horrified at Billy's behaviour – in fact, I think he was very much against the engagement altogether, but Billy was well educated, gentlemanly, and made a good deal of money, and though Mr Stanfield was a rich man he could not raise any reasonable objection to the match, for Billy and Mona were very much in love with each other.

---

[163] Boxer.

Well, Mr Stanfield told Billy he'd like a few words with him, and poor Billy, looking very much ashamed of himself, followed his prospective father-in-law. Mr Stanfield told Billy that he was ashamed to see that he had no more dignity than to be skylarking with common sailors. Billy answered that he was nothing but a common sailor himself, which he (Mr Stanfield) had known all along.

Mr Stanfield said: 'Yes, I was aware that in one sense you are only a common sailor, but in another you are very different, but now I insist that the engagement before existing between my daughter and yourself must be at an end.'

Poor old Billy said that he was very sorry, but that he thought it rather hard that a bit of a boyish frolic should be the means of spoiling his life; and he did plead hard too, in his honest boyish fashion, and as a man can when he is in love.

But it was like trying to get blood out of a stone, trying to make the old gentleman give in, or overlook poor Bill's love of fun. No, his pride was more to him than anyone else's anguish, and Bill and Mona did suffer too.

Tears and prayer were alike of no use from either of them, and they were so young too. I do think he might have forgiven Billy. But he was as proud as Lucifer, and told Billy that HIS daughter should never wed a low buffoon.

It is getting very late now boys. I will finish telling you about Billy another time."

# Chapter 37

## *A Tasmanian Episode*

"Grandfather," said Jack, "you haven't told us a yarn for ever so long. I've just been reading a grand yarn about Brady and McCabe[164], the Tasmanian bushrangers. Do you know anything about them? Tell us if you do."

"Yes do tell us Grandfather," we all cried.

"Well boys, I can't tell you much that is not known to you already about the men. I saw McCabe several times, but never saw Brady. We went out to see McCabe brought in, when he was taken – a lot of schoolboys, heartless schoolboys they called us – but we were far from heartless, though our curiosity led us a good deal out of the way to see this unfortunate man.

We went to Wellington Bridge, a good many of us, because we knew we'd get a good look at him as he passed over it. Presently they came, a body of the mounted police, but McCabe was on foot, hand-cuffed to a policeman. He was a tall, fine-looking fellow with rather a sad face. The boys felt inclined to cheer, not that they were glad he was taken, but because they, like all boys of that age, admired the courage and coolness of the man, for though his energies were wrongly directed, he had the cause of the wronged and the oppressed really at heart, and we boys knew it.

He knew too, why we had come out there to meet him, and he gave us a smile and a nod; that smile made me as sad as I ever felt, and more than one of us burst into sobs.

We were only small boys then, but living as we did in the midst of it all, we understood, young and all as we were.

---

[164]James McCabe and Matthew Brady were leaders of a notorious Tasmanian bushranger gang in the 1820s.

I felt miserable enough the day of the execution too. I wasn't more than twelve years old, but even now I hate to think of it. There is something in the hush of a great crowd gathered to see anything of that sort than in anything else I know of. Everyone seems to hold their breath – a shiver, a sob, a groan runs through the whole multitude.

What a moment before was a moving, living mass, talking, nursing, laughing, swearing, some dissenting, others agreeing with the sentence to be carried out, had in one instant become as one man, silent and motionless, every nerve strained to its utmost tension. Expectation, horror, fear, brutal delight can be traced on the faces of the motley throng; each in a characteristic way shows how it affects him, and yet there is that sudden pause and hush that makes the many one. It is as if they paused to let the Great Presence, Death, pass through on its way to the gallows.

It is a fearful sight, and I often wonder now how it was that people crowded in such numbers to see such a crowded spectacle. Young and old, rich and poor, innocent and sin-hardened, they all alike seemed fascinated by the sight of a fellow-creature being swung into eternity.

There is the religious ritual – often the prisoners themselves, if there were many, sang hymns up to the last. Then there is the low murmur of the parson's or priest's (whichever the case may be) voice, the sergeant's short, concise declaration, the prisoner's final words, if he cares to say anything. Then comes the hangman's task – the rope is fixed, the drop is lowered, and there is a dull thud, felt rather than heard – and all is over.

Then once more the people are the people, moving and living again in a moment, some talking and laughing as if nothing had happened, others denouncing the authorities, others, generally the worst amongst them, declaring that they had got their desserts, women and children sobbing and weeping. Some whose curiosity was strong, would fight for places near the gallows, where they could watch the face of the prisoner turn from dull red to death's blue, see the glassy eyes glare and the jaw drop.

It was a fearful, ghastly sight and the prisoners died in such different moods, most of them as they had lived; some set their teeth and died hard; others again were hysterical and lost all self-control, other bragging and indifferent, some mirthful and apparently in good humour; others resigned, pathetic and repentant, some innocent and pleading for mercy, while others again cursed God and died."

James McCabe, Tasmanian Bushranger. Unknown artist.

# Chapter 38

## BILLY MANSFIELD AND MONA

"Grandfather, please go on telling us about Billy Mansfield and Mona will you?" said Jack.

"Yes my boy. I told you that Mona's father refused to allow Billy to marry her. The poor fellow was dreadfully cut up about it, for he knew that Mona was suffering too, through his thoughtlessness. He asked to see Mona to say goodbye, but even that was denied him.

'The old fellow is her father,' he said to me, 'and I suppose he has some right to dispose of his daughter as he likes, but he's going a trifle too far I fancy, and he'll be sorry for it someday I think. Of course I can't marry Mona now, but at least I can see her again, and I WILL. You'll help me won't you?' he added.

I agreed without a moment's hesitation, and I called the old gentleman every name I could think of, and though Billy pretended to protest, I was sure he agreed with me, and it comforted him to hear me put into words what his respect for Mona's father would not let him utter.

Well, we managed that interview – never mind how, and Bill and Mona saw each other for the last time. As we were in a boat, I had to be present, but they didn't mind me, and I tried hard not to hear or see.

It was terrible to see her distress, and she was so pretty too. She clung so to big handsome Billy, who looked the picture of misery too.

Mona offered to run away with him then, but he told her in a heartbroken voice that he couldn't let her do anything she might regret all her life.

All the same it would have been much better if she had done so; but Billy's sense of honour was too fine to take advantage of the love of a young girl – almost a child.

And so they parted. It was indeed one of those partings 'such as crush the life from out young hearts.[165]' Poor Bill! I felt almost as miserable about it as he did.

If things had gone smoothly I believe her refining influence would have done great things for Billy. As it was – to his credit be it said – he did not go to the bad, as more than one of us expected. He was always the same faithful chum, the same affectionate son and brother as long as I could keep trace of him.

As for poor Mona, her life was one long misery after that. Her home had never been one of the happiest – that was the reason, I think, she clung so to Billy, and the reason that I regretted his rather strained sense of honour. Her step-mother was forever taunting her about her 'sailor whaler' as she styled Billy, till the poor girl was nearly crazy.

When she grew older every influence was brought to bear, and she was goaded into marrying a vulgar wealthy farmer – a man older than her own father. He was very jealous and exacting to a degree, and led her an awful life.

Mona didn't live very long after her marriage. She wrote once to me, saying that she was glad to die, and entrusting me with a letter and a ring for her dear Billy.

And so I knew that she never ceased to care for Billy. A long time afterwards I was able to send the small packet to him, for I was never sure of his whereabouts before, and I did not want it to go astray.

As for poor Billy, he never married."

---

[165] William is quoting *The Hunted Outlaw, Donald Morrison, the Canadian Rob Roy*. By Anonymous, 1889.

# Chapter 39

## DEATH OF A VETERAN – "BUCK" WATSON – OLD BOOTI

"Grandfather," said Jack, "I saw in the Western Star that an old man named Watson had died at Riverton the other day, aged 92. Did you know him?"

"Know him? I should think so my boy. 'Old Buck' we used to call him. Just fancy his being dead now. I remember he came down here whaling in '39. He only whaled one season though and that was enough for him.

He was whaling in the *Scotia* for Johnny Jones. One day they were putting ballast aboard when one of the boats swamped and sank. They could see the boat lying in the river (it happened to be Riverton), and Jones said;

'You can have that boat Buck, if you can get her up.'

So Buck dived and dived until he got all the stones out of the boat. Then he painted her up and got her all trim, and the next time Jones came to Jacob's River and saw his old boat, he rather repented his generosity, so he asked Buck if he would take a cask of brandy for the boat.

Buck agreed and that was the beginning of his hotel keeping. I don't know where that brandy came from, but it was the vilest stuff I ever came across, and yet he got 4/- per quart, or 1/- for half a pint of it.

He used to keep the liquor in a little storehouse away from his house and he had such a big dog chained there to guard the brandy; but in spite of the dog, some fellows managed to get a key and stole some of the brandy. When that was all gone, Buck used to walk to the New River to get five gallons of whiskey from a man who had a private still there[166].

---

[166] Probably from ex-whaler Owen McShane of Sandy Point. McShane was a sly brewer of a notoriously strong brand of distilled cabbage tree rum.

This man used to brew a good deal in those days, till Mr Mantell came down and overhauled his place. Then he sold his plant and it was moved down to the Toi tois[167].

He was a steady, careful man, was Buck. He got some cattle once from old Booti, and started cattle rearing and did pretty well too. Poor old Booti was an Otaheati man[168]. He was a grand old chap too. He was our cook and steward in the old *Kairari*, and many a lark we had with old Booti. The way he managed to get the cattle down to New Zealand was rather remarkable.

One day, in Twofold Bay, Captain Howell was loading the *Kairari* with different goods he had bought from a man named Boyd, and the things were alongside in Boyd's hulk. In slinging a cask of nails the rope slipped and down they went to the bottom. Captain Howell was very vexed about it, as the nails were expensive, and as they were all sizes would have been useful in New Zealand just at that time.

Strange to say, though the head was out of the cask, not a single nail was spilt the water was perfectly clear, and down old Booti went to see what he could do to recover the nails. He came up and got the rope he wanted, and told them that as soon as he pulled the rope to draw up as quickly as possible. Down he went again and fastened on his rope, and he never broke water until the nails were safely hauled up; but when he did appear, blood was pouring from his nose, mouth and ears.

The other men declared that they would not have gone down there for a cask of nails. But Captain Howell was pleased and gave Booti some cattle, and brought them down here for him, and then Booti sold them to Buck Watson.

I remember we were sailing the west side in the *Kairari*, and one day we were in a great hurry to get our dinner. Old Booti was bustling round in a great state, and

---

[167] Fortrose, eastern Southland.

[168] From Tahiti.

he asked George Stevens[169] – 'Tukunini' we used to call him – to go and get him a 'lish' – dish he meant. Tukunini pretended he could not understand what he wanted and off old Booti flew in such a rage, and coming back banged Tukunini on the head shouting, 'Lish, lish, lish!' till the bottom fell out of the dish. We did laugh, and Captain Howell roared and said,

'That's just what he wanted Booti,' but Tukunini never tried any of his tricks on old Booti again.

Poor old Booti lost his wife in Easy Harbour on the S.W. side of Stewart Island. Captain Wiseman was taking the Codfish people to the Chatham Islands. A strong N.W. gale sprang up and Tommy Chasland, who was on board, took the *Industry*, as the ship was called, into Easy Harbour; but the captain was afraid there was a rocky bottom or something and he determined to go out again.

Just as they were going out the mate called out, 'Breakers ahead!'

'No such thing,' said Tommy, 'it is just the rip of the sea, and if you turn round to go back into the harbour now, you are lost.'

But the Captain would not listen to Tom, and turned round to go back. There was a fearful wind blowing and the main-topsail sheet was carried away, and away the vessel went. Geo. Moss said that he just put his hand on her foretack, ran down her stern and got ashore dry footed.

Tommy Chasland got a fearful gash in the skull – half of it would have killed any other man but Tommy. Poor old Booti got himself out all right, but he went in three times for his wife. He said he could have got her out all right too, only that every time he got into the kelp she let go of him. He had no clothes on for her to clutch hold of, and she was pretty well worn out, and poor Booti couldn't hold her and fight the water at the same time, so in front of his eyes he saw his wife drown, and he was awfully cut up about it, poor fellow. He was killed some time afterwards himself. They were working at Mr Howell's vessel, the *Amazon*. Booti was down below digging out, as they thought she wasn't going to float off

---

[169] Captain Howell's half brother.

easily. A half-drunken Yankee named Bill Roe was up above knocking down the shores. He hit Booti on the head and he died shortly afterwards.

The Maoris were exceedingly fond of Booti, and we had a great hob to keep them from killing Bill Roe. We buried poor old Booti just near the big boatshed round at Tall's Point. A countryman of his with his wife and children, is buried close beside him; their name was Gregory."

Whaling at Twofold Bay, mid 19th century. O. W. Brierly Collection.

# Chapter 40

## THE PILOT'S DAUGHTER

"Grandfather, do tell us a yarn," said Fred.

"Yes do Grandfather," said Tom, "and let it have a love story."

Now Tom is eighteen and falls in love on an average of once a week, so of course we all roared; but Grandfather who wanted to please Tom, promised to tell us a love story, much to the disgust of Fred, and Jack began to spout the inevitable Lindsay Gordon:

> *"I loved a girl not long ago,*
>
> *And till my suit was told*
>
> *I thought her breast was white as snow —*
>
> *'Twas very near as cold."*

"Well boys, if I am to tell you a story you had better let me begin, and stop quarrelling among yourselves. If Fred objects to love stories he had better go away, and Jack can have the floor for Lindsay Gordon afterwards."

"Well," said Grandfather, "I will tell you about a clerk that Bloody Jack had. He brought him over from Sydney and he stayed in New Zealand for a good while. His name was Escott – Duke Escott, they used to call him, though he had no right to the title.

He was not a bad looking fellow, and very well educated. He was manager of a branch of his uncle's business, something to do with a colliery, in a seaport town in the North of England. While there he became acquainted with a young and beautiful girl named Margery Graham, the daughter of a pilot.

The girl was young and foolish; her mother had died years before, and she was the pride and delight of her father's heart. He gave her every advantage he could, sent her to a good school where, as she was quick and intelligent, she received a fair education, but she had a taste for life above her father's position, and when she went home again, instead of the affectionate daughter the poor old father expected to see, he was met by a very stylish young lady with most extravagant ideas, and she on her part felt dissatisfied with her life, disgusted with what she termed her father's vulgarity, and her affection was not strong enough for her to put her own wishes in the background and study to be a cheerful and contented for her father's sake. She fretted and grumbled till her father remarked to a neighbour.

'That darned school has took all the goodness out of my gal.'

One day the spoilt beauty was wandering aimlessly about the beach as usual bemoaning her hard lot to a very appreciative audience – herself. She refused to be friendly with those who tried to show her any kindness and of course those she wished to mix with would not associate with her.

She was taking her usual solitary walk when in rounding a sudden curve she met a young fellow in boating flannels evidently on pleasure bent. He raised his hat as he came up to her and asked her if she could show him the nearest way to the boatsheds where the watermen had pleasure boats for hire.

She showed him, of course, and with a few words of thanks he was gone. Meanwhile Margery thought to herself that he must be the new manager she had heard her father talking about, and at once life assumed a new interest to her, and on the spot she determined to marry him. The task that she set herself was not a difficult one – that of captivating the young man.

Now Escott was not strictly handsome, but was a fine specimen of manhood nevertheless – one of those stalwart, wholesome looking fair young Englishmen that one seems to trust instinctively.

He was just at the age too, when he thought all women were angels, and almost at once fell head over ears in love with the pretty, but shallow, Margery Graham.

She knew her young lover better than he knew himself and never allowed her shallow-mindedness to appear when he was with her, never fretted and grumbled, was pensive and sad, pretended to be poetical and have longings for a higher life than she led. Each day young Escott thought the little minx more fascinating. He always shared her walks now, brought her books and songs and flattered her to the top of her bent. At last they were engaged, though the little deceiver had made a fine show of giving him up because of her inferior birth and position, which of course she knew would strengthen his determination to marry her, and so he was going to do in spite of his relations.

His mother and sisters, who were honestly determined to make the best of it, came down to see his future bride, and they saw her as she was too – empty headed and vain. They were cut up about it, as was natural, and not all Miss Margery's little witcheries could blind them, or lead them for one moment to suppose that she loved Duke. One day they were all sitting on the beach when Blanche, Duke's second sister, remarked,

'Did you know Duke, that old Uncle James is dead, and has left all his money to his doctor and housekeeper, so you won't have it after all, and will have nothing to live on. Uncle James did always say he intended to make you his heir too.'

This was a little experiment on the part of the sisters, as they wanted to show Margery in her true colours to their brother. It was true about the money too, and they waited a little anxiously to see what would happen next. Duke turned rather pale for a moment and then he declared he did not care as long as he had his wife.

'But I do care,' snapped Margery, 'and you have been deceiving me you wretch. You always said you would be rich when your uncle died. I won't marry you now, and you needn't expect it.'

Poor Escott was too astonished to realise that this outraged, coarse minded woman was the same gentle, loving creature of an hour before; but his sisters expected nothing else, for they had been astonished and disgusted many a time to hear the cool way in which Margery talked about 'when we get our money.'

That very day Margery ran off with a rich but very disreputable old man, who had long admired her pretty face. I don't know what became of her, but her chances of happiness would be small indeed.

As for Escott, he was so nearly crazy. He was angry with his mother, his sisters, his uncle, Margery, all in turn. Poor old Graham too, was in a great state. He came to Escott next day looking old and haggard, but honest and true as usual.

'I'm sorry for thee lad,' he said, 'but don't blame the lass too much. It was all that darned boarding school – and she had no mother.' The poor old fellow broke down with the last words and Escott forgot some of his own misery in trying to comfort Margery's father.

Escott had no money, but he determined to leave England, and took the first chance he could of taking himself off. He wouldn't wait to be helped by anyone but went away without a word of warning as a valet to Lord Byron, who was then travelling about on the Continent.

He had knocked about the world a lot. He was a clever man too, but fearfully bitter and hard in speaking about women – he judged them all by one unworthy specimen. After he left New Zealand he went to Manila, but he interfered with the religion of the people or something – anyway the Government gave him so long to leave the place Captain King gave him passage to England in the *Annette*, and the last I heard of him he was going from bad to worse in London, and all for the sake of a women's false and pretty face."

# *THE END*

# Bibliography

## Original records

Births, deaths, and marriages New Zealand www.dia.govt.nz/Births-deaths-and-marriages

Invercargill City Council and Southland District Council cemeteries databases.
Southland Times and Otago Witness from paperspast.natlib.govt.nz

Letter from Mr William Thomas to Theophilus Daniel, April 25th 1884. (Misc-MS-1988), Hocken Library

Misc. Papers pertaining to Native reserves (MA-MT 6 Box 15), Archives New Zealand

Whakapapa book containing details of William Thomas and Mary Tukewaha. (MS-2431/070), Hocken Library

## Secondary sources

Anderson, A. *Te Puoho's last raid*. Otago Heritage Books, Dunedin, 1986

Beattie, J. H. 1949. *The Maoris of Fiordland. The Maoris and Fiordland: Maori myths, fascinating fables, legendary lore, typical traditions and native nomenclature*. Otago Daily Times and Witness, Dunedin.

Beattie, J.H. 1950. *Far famed Fiordland: historic and descriptive : European explorers, white whalers, seamen and surveyors, travellers and tourists, and Pakeha place-names*. Otago Daily Times and Witness, Dunedin.

Beattie, J.H. 1994. *Māori lore of lake, alp and fiord: folk lore, fairy tales, traditions and place-names of the scenic wonderland of the South Island*. Reprint Cadsonbury Publications, Christchurch.

Calder, J.E. 1873. *'Illustrated by a Sketch of the Career of Michael Howe' in Historical Records of Australia*, series 3, vol 2. Mercury, Hobart.

Coutts, Peter. 1972. *The emergence of the Foveaux Strait Maori from prehistory*. PhD Thesis. University of Otago, Dunedin.

Cyclopedia Co. 1905. *Cyclopedia of New Zealand: Otago and Southland Provincial Districts*. Cyclopedia Co., Wellington.

Dakin, William, J. 2000. *Whalemen adventures: the story of whaling in Australian waters and other southern seas related thereto, from the days of sails to modern times*. Facsimile by Kiwi Publishers, Christchurch.

Grady, Don. 1986. *Sealers & Whalers in New Zealand waters*. Reed Methuen, Auckland.

Hall-Jones, J. 1979. *The South Explored*. A.H. & A.W. Reed, Wellington.

Hall-Jones, J. 2002. *The Fjords of Fiordland*. Craig Printing Co., Invercargill.

Hocken, Thomas. 1898. *Contributions to the early history of New Zealand*. Sampson Low, London.

McNab, Robert. 1913. *The old whaling days: a history of southern New Zealand from 1830 to 1840*. Whitcombe & Tombs, Christchurch.

Morton, Harry. 1982. *The whaler's wake*. University of Otago Press, Dunedin.

Prickett, Nigel. 2002. *The archaeology of New Zealand shore whaling*. Department of Conservation, Wellington.

Pybus, T.A. 1954. *The Maoris of the South Island*. Reed Publishing, Wellington.

Richards, Rhys, 1995. *The Foveaux whaling yarns of Yankee Jack: Burr Osborn's adventures in southern New Zealand, 1845*. Otago Heritage Books, Dunedin.

Richards, Rhys 1995. *Murihiku' re-viewed : a revised history of Southern New Zealand from 1804 to 1844*. Lithographic Services, Wellington.

Smith, Graham. 1984. *Thomas – Tukuwaha: A record of the families 1834 – 1984*. Hamilton.
Smith, Ian. 2002. *The New Zealand sealing industry: history, archaeology, and heritage management*. Department of Conservation, Wellington.

Stevens, Kate, 2008. *Gathering Places: the mixed descent families of Foveaux Strait and Rakiura/Stewart Island, 1824-1864*, Unpublished BA(Hons) History dissertation, University of Otago.

Tau, Te Maire and Anderson, Atholl (eds.). 2008. *Ngāi Tahu : a migration history: the Carrington text*. Bridget Williams Books ; Christchurch

Tregear, E. (1885). *The Aryan Maori* (pp. 7-17, 81-96). Wellington, New Zealand: George Didsbury, Government Printer.

Waite, Fred. 1948. *Pioneering in South Otago*. Otago Centennial Publications.

# Appendix 1:

## THOMAS – TUKUWAHA WHAKAPAPA

William (**Bill**) Thomas m. **Tukuwaha**/Mary (married in 1834)

    William Thomas Jnr. b.1835

    Mary b.1836/7

    Jane b.1838

    Elizabeth b.1842

    Charles b. 1846

    John b.1848

    George b. 14.4.1851

    **Emma** b. 23.5.1853 married John Nonnet Simon

        **Caroline** (Lillie) Georgina De Peracene (b. 1874.)

        Henry Tom (**Tom**) b. 1876

        Marianne Schlotelle b.1878

        Louis Michael Herman b.1880 d.1887

        John Powell (**Jack**) b.1881

        Alfred Rupert (**Fred**) b.1883

        Maria Emma Dora b.1884

        Leionie Gertrude de Zoete b.1886

        Annie Victoria Mervyn b.1887

        Catherine Edith b.1888

        Faulkner Charles Roy (**Bertie**) b.1891

        Max Augustus Sedgley b.1894

        Caroline b. 1854, d.1868

        Francis b. 3.7.1856, d.1861

Note: people that feature in the narrative are highlighted in bold. A full genealogy can be found in *Thomas – Tukuwaha: A record of the families 1834 – 1984*. Tukuwaha was buried in the old cemetery at Riverton and William Thomas and many of the Simon branch of the family were buried in a communal plot in the Invercargill Eastern Cemetery Block 10 Plot 131A.

# Index

# Image Credits

**Cover** *Oreti Beach.* Strawberry Mouse 2011. Courtesy Strawberry Mouse Design, Invercargill

**Page 9** *John Nonnet Simon and Emma Simon (nee Thomas).* Courtesy the Thomas family, Invercargill

**Page 14** *William Thomas Junior.* Courtesy the Thomas family, Invercargill

**Page 21** *Weller Bros. Whaling Station, Otakou.* After A Coville, mid 19th century. Original painting courtesy the Otago Settlers Museum, Dunedin

**Page 26** *Tuhawaiki's moko.* After Tuhawaiki, 1840. Original image courtesy Hocken Library, Dunedin

**Page 32** *Edward Weller.* Original photograph courtesy the Otago Settlers Museum, Dunedin

**Page 34** *Cutting in a Whale.* Unknown photographer, 1903. Courtesy of Curious Expeditions.

**Page 38** *Makariri.* Original photograph courtesy the Otago Settlers Museum, Dunedin

**Page 45** *Breaksea Sound.* Photograph by Guy, c. 1905. From Cyclopedia of New Zealand Otago/Southland edition, 1905.

**Page 58** *Sarah's Bosom. Port Ross, Auckland Islands.* After Le Breton, 1842. Original image courtesy National Library of Australia.

**Page 61** *Edwin Palmer.* Original photograph courtesy the Otago Settlers Museum, Dunedin

**Page 64** *Elizabeth 'Betty' Guard.* Silhouette courtesy of the Guard family (after the original held by Te Papa, F.003557)

**Page 73** *Te Rauparaha.* After Charles Heaphy, 1839. Courtesy T. McGee. Unknown where original image is held.

**Page 80** *Mermaid at Oyster Bay, 1818.* From Captain King 'Narrative of a Survey", John Murray, London, 1822. Unknown where original image is held.

**Page 88** *Captain John Lort Stokes.* After William Egley, 1864. Original image held by Australian National Library.

**Page 92** *Chief Wakataupuka.* After John Boultbee, 1827. Image courtesy Alexander Turnbull Library, Wellington.

**Page 104** *Whaling Port, Bay of Islands.* Unknown artist, c. mid 19th century. Unknown where original image is held.

**Page 107** *Sydney Gallows.* Unknown artist, c. 19th century. Unknown where original image is held.

**Page 129** *Lt. Colonel George Johnson.* Unknown artist, 1810. Based on an image held by the State Library of New South Wales.

**Page 134** *Governor Lachlan Macquarie and Elizabeth Macquarie.* After A. Garran 1888. Unknown where original image is held.

**Page 138** *Captain Kelly.* Unknown artist, c. 1820s. After K. Bowden. Unknown where original is held.

**Page 158** *Bishop Selwyn.* Unknown artist, c. 1840s. Unknown where original is held.

**Page 167** *James McCabe.* Unknown artist, c. 1820s. Unknown where original is held.

**Page 173** *Whaling at Twofold Bay*, mid 19th century. O.W. Brierly Collection.

www.ingramcontent.com/pod-product-compliance
Lightning Source LLC
Chambersburg PA
CBHW080612270326
41928CB00016B/3031